Teaching
and Learning
in Multicultural
Classrooms

Teaching
and Learning
in Multicultural
Classrooms

Paul Gardner

David Fulton Publishers
London

David Fulton Publishers Ltd
The Chiswick Centre, 414 Chiswick High Road, London W4 5TF
www.fultonpublishers.co.uk

First published in Great Britain in 2001 by David Fulton Publishers

Note: The rights of Paul Gardner to be identified as the author of this work
have been asserted by him in accordance with the Copyright, Designs and
Patents Act 1988.

David Fulton Publishers is a division of Granada Learning Limited, part of
Granada plc.

British Library Cataloguing in Publication Data
A catalogue record for this book is available from the British Library.

ISBN 1-85346-710-3

Typeset by Textype Typesetters, Cambridge
Printed and bound in Great Britain

Contents

Acknowledgements

A book is never the work of a single person only. The text emerges from interactions with others. I would, therefore, like to thank a number of people for giving me their time and sharing their experiences with me: Judith Sampson; Anne McCormick; Asha Gulati; Roshan Jawad; Sue Crabbe.

I would also like to extend my thanks to the following students at De Montfort University for their help: Kiranjeet Dhanjal; Kulbir Bansal; Alev Ibrahim; Juleanne Skeete; Ranjit Kaur.

Finally, a special thank you to my colleagues in the primary team of the School of Education at De Montfort University for their support and encouragement during this project.

Introduction

'Education influences and reflects the values of society, and the kind of society we want to be.' (DfEE/QCA 1999a: 10)

'It is inconceivable that any pupil currently in school could live their life without meeting, working with, or in some other way affecting or being affected by, people from a wide range of different ethnic backgrounds.' (Gillborn and Mirza 2000: 6)

The first of the above statements, which implies the symbiotic relationship of education and society, comes from the introduction to the revised National Curriculum 2000. Inherent to the second statement is the relevance of multi-cultural education to classrooms in every school in the land. It comes from a DfEE report entitled *Educational Inequality*. Taken together, the two statements highlight education's social and cultural functions and the importance of consensual values in a pluralist society. If we start from the premise that Britain is a complex, post-colonial, multicultural society, consisting of diverse systems of belief, family patterns, modes of behaviour and interpersonal relations, the statements fore-shadow the task ahead for us as a society and for education as a constituent part of society. Essential to the task is a school's ability to enable individual pupils to value and respect their own cultural heritage while simultaneously helping them to understand cultures different from their own. In essence, schools must reflect diversity within an inclusive ethos.

However, part of that inclusiveness is the ability to be responsive to the dynamic nature of culture and cross-cultural influence. A culture is not static and to treat it as such risks casting its members as stereotypes because stereotype refuses to acknowledge difference. Unfortunately, stereotypes are prevalent in our society and perpetuate superficial representations and misconceptions of social groups, to the extent that individuality is subsumed within an erroneous set of simplified characteristics. Stereotypes can be sustained by such things as newspaper headlines, visual images, the claims of politicians and the discourse of everyday life in which conversation, comment and humour play their part. Stereotype is the companion to prejudice, bigotry, racism, and social exclusion. These are tensions that provide us, as educators, with major obstacles as we implement equal opportunity policies and practices. They force us to ask important questions about the kind of society we are and want to be.

Inherent to a society's culture is not only its values, traditions and heritage, but also the perceptions it has of itself and the view it has of the world, if we can determine what kind of a society we are and want to be, if we have a consensus about what we want to preserve and what needs changing, then the sociological function of education is made a little simpler. While members of a society may share things in common, advanced post-industrial societies such as ours provide a kaleidoscope of social experience for their various members. The individual's view of society is likely to be bound within his or her subjective experience as a member of that society. Such experience involves both the individual's interaction with the social world and his or her interpretation of that social world. Interpretations of social experience are likely to be channelled along the axes of class, gender, 'race', ethnicity and disability, which position us as members of groups and as individuals in relation to the material and symbolic order of society. The multicultural classroom, therefore, has to accommodate the development of individual, as well as group identities, and enable an understanding of the processes that shape us, while recognising the individual as an agent of choice.

At the beginning of the 21st century then, schools are, as they always have been, important centres for the processing of social values. At the heart of this book is a consideration of important questions education must answer if we are to shape the kind of social values necessary for a well-knit multicultural society. These questions include such things as: how can we create an inclusive education, one that acknowledges the obvious difference and diversity that exist within our society? How can we respond sensitively to the particular needs and experiences of different groups? How can we defeat stereotype and its attendant vices by recognising that groups are made up of individuals with their own unique ways of seeing and doing? How can we cross the attitudinal Rubicon to the point where equality does not mean we are all the same? Perhaps the essential question and the one that has taxed us the most is: how can we improve the life chances of our most disadvantaged pupils by raising their levels of academic achievement and feeling of self-worth? The real answers to these questions will be found in what happens in individual classrooms, not in policy statements.

Throughout the book I have tried to reflect what has happened, or is happening now, in the field of multicultural education, by grounding work in practical experience. The relationship between education and society and the changing perspectives of society in relation to itself are important features of Chapter One, which charts the development of multicultural education within the evolution of Britain as a multicultural society. By giving the reader a brief historical backdrop to multicultural education the intention is to set the context for what has followed.

Chapter Two begins with an investigation of the extent to which educational policy for multicultural education influenced what happened in some multi-ethnic schools during the 1990s. The second half of the chapter draws on the programmes of study of Curriculum 2000 to propose possible future directions for a multicultural curriculum.

During the 1990s and into the 21st century disparity of academic outcomes between different ethnic groups became a national concern, prompting several investigations of school effectiveness. Through a summary of the main findings of the reports that followed these investigations, Chapter Three highlights a raft of measures that multicultural schools might implement to raise achievement. Chapter Four is a companion to Chapter Three in that it explores, through case study, two successful multicultural schools and helps to put the findings, discussed in the previous chapter, into a practical context.

Language is central to education and is the medium through which values, status and identity materialise. The development of language in multicultural classrooms is, therefore, central to any discussion of teaching and learning. Chapter Five explores the power of language, both as a positive and as a negative force. The process of acquiring additional languages is outlined and collaborative learning is discussed as a means of accelerating understanding both of the curriculum and of learners themselves.

The final chapter focuses on the importance of developing shared aims and approaches between colleagues in the classroom, and between home and school, in pursuit of effective teaching and learning.

The classroom is a critical social arena where individual lives are shaped and influenced through attitudes and values, which are embedded in both the content and processes of learning. High expectations, positive values and an inclusive ethos, that is, an acceptance and conceptual understanding of difference, are the guardians of success. They enable individuals, as well as social and ethnic groups, to achieve academic success. They also influence self-worth, hope and optimism; the kind of emotional balance that leads to positive relationships built on empathy. In the past, we have often failed to create a fully inclusive education to meet the needs of our multicultural society. By surveying the past and projecting into the future I hope to provide the reader with a critical view of teaching and learning in multicultural classrooms; one that will enable professional decisions to be made with confidence.

Dedication

To Tajinder, Ashrup and Nanaki. For your love, warmth and joy.

CHAPTER 1

Changing perspectives in multicultural education

Educational change rarely occurs because of isolated events and can usually be linked to wider social and economic change; political imperative; technological and cultural innovation, and fresh ways of thinking about how best to organise teaching and learning. This link between education and society, between the needs of the individual and the needs of the wider social world, is now readily recognised and has been made explicit in the introduction to the new National Curriculum (DfEE/QCA 1999a and b: 10).

The symbiotic relationship between education and a society that became visibly more multicultural during the second half of the 20th century is also apparent in the way minority ethnic pupils have been viewed and provided for in British schools. In telling the story of this provision it will be necessary to reflect some parallel developments in political thinking and in social attitudes. In turn, these have come under the influence of the ebb and flow of the economy in the post-war period with concomitant influences on, and by, migration, both within and across the borders of the British Isles. It is not my intention to explore in depth the factors that have caused migration to Britain from around the world. I start from the position that migration was and still is a social and economic fact. My initial intention is to look at how early migration and prevailing social and political attitudes influenced educational provision for minority ethnic pupils and then consider how perceptions of Britain as a multicultural society began to change our views, not only about how the needs of minority ethnic pupils should be met, but also about the general nature of what constituted an appropriate education for a multi-ethnic society. This chapter then charts the development of educational provision by the state for minority ethnic pupils from the 1960s to April 2000, the date on which Government grant for raising achievement of minority ethnic pupils was devolved directly to schools, as part of the Standards Fund.

Migration and change

The history of Britain might be described as the history of a relatively small group of islands that has been shaped by the cultures of settlers from numerous other places. Its earliest inhabitants may have had links with people in the Mediterranean and the Near East (CRE 1996: 7). From the earliest times, waves of migration have brought significant technological, economic and cultural change that has helped shape the people we are today. One of the most significant advances was the knowledge of how to cultivate crops and domesticate animals. This knowledge was brought to these islands by the Celts, who originated in Central Europe, an area now comprising the Czech and Slovak Republics, Hungary, Austria, Switzerland and parts of southern Germany (Chadwick 1970: 18–19).

The economic legacy of the Romans, who finally settled in Britain following their third invasion in 43AD is evident in some of our road networks and settlements, among other things. Because the Roman army included soldiers from many parts of its Empire, Roman Britain, like the Britain of today, was a multiracial society (Fryer 1984: 1). Numerous other settlers, including the Saxons, Danes and Normans made significant contributions to the development of our language and culture. We have a history that has provided us with the rich legacy of diversity. It is a fact we sometimes neglect and need to draw more attention to as an important characteristic of our national identity, rather than trying to pretend we are a monocultural society.

The history curriculum in English primary schools deals with the chronology of the arrival of these and other invaders and settlers. However, there is a danger that if the curriculum does not include due recognition of the breadth of migration of people, ideas, goods and technology, from around the world to these shores, it will be reduced to a minimalist Europeanised historical perspective. Fryer (1984) has documented the presence in Britain of African, Indian and other migrant groups and their contributions to British society throughout its history. Teachers and students will need to do their research in order to fulfil all the requirements of the programme of study in history at Key Stages 2 and 3, in particular, the requirement that: 'Pupils should be taught about the social, cultural, religious and ethnic diversity of the societies studied, in Britain and the wider world . . .' (DfEE/QCA 1999a: 105, H2b; DfEE/QCA 1999b: 150, H2b)

Much of this information about our multicultural history has been collated in the relatively recent past, during the 1980s and 1990s. It is perhaps a function of the need to affirm the presence of Black Britons against the insularity of some White Britons who hold erroneous views of their own history. Similarly, feminist scholars and left-wing historians have revealed that woman and working class people, respectively, have largely been 'hidden' from history but were, in fact, significant contributors to it (Spender 1982; Thompson 1991; Hill 1991). Through the assiduous work of dedicated people who have asked searching questions, we are in the process of discovering more about ourselves. Fresh findings have implications for the curriculum. As Gaine and George (1999: 68) point out, the 'curriculum is where a society . . . tries to embody its own sense of itself'. That sense of self, reflected in curriculum content, is dependent upon whose view is being represented. Clearly then, in culturally diverse, democratic societies there are many groups that have a stake in what the curriculum should look like. The extent to which the National Curriculum is a true reflection of British society is an issue I shall return to in Chapter Two. In the recent past British governments have shown, at best, an ambivalent attitude to migration and at worst, a hostile one. Changing attitudes and accompanying discourses have influenced the development of educational responses to ethnic diversity in Britain.

Migration, economy and racism

What has characterised post-war migration and makes it distinctly different from previous migration is that the peoples who have made Britain their home have come from widespread geographic backgrounds but, like other groups, they have helped to 'revitalise and transform Britain' (Panayi 1999). Panayi identifies three phases in this post-war migration. Firstly, labour shortages, following the cessation of conflict in 1945, encouraged the recruitment of Southern and Eastern Europeans to the workforce. Some of these new recruits were already here in displaced people's camps. Secondly, as the flow of labour from continental Europe and Ireland began to dwindle, fresh sources of labour were sought in the countries of the Empire and the Commonwealth. Many thousands of Caribbean, African and Asian servicemen had fought as British and Commonwealth recruits during the war and Britain was still viewed across vast tracts of the globe as the 'Mother Country.' Thirdly, and as a result of racial prejudice, the Government of 1962 took measures to restrict the entry of non-white migrants to Britain. Implicit to this illustration of Panayi's phases of post-war migration is the tension between, on the one hand, Britain's changing economic circumstances and, on the other, a racism that has deep historic origins and was, and still is, grounded in erroneous perceptions of colour. The experience of those early migrants and the difficulties they encountered in employment and housing has been recorded in perpetuity by several Black writers of the time. Two such writers were Edward Braithwaite, from Guyana, and Wole Soyinka, from Nigeria. Braithwaite had served in the RAF during the war and his novel, *Reluctant Neighbours*, recalls his attempts to find work here. In the following extract he converses with an American he has befriended during a train journey.

'Did you teach college level?' my neighbour asked.

'No. Secondary School.'

'Any problem about your colour?' he asked.

'My colour is always a problem. For some people.' I wondered if he was trying slyly to needle me . . .

'Were you the only black teacher in the school?'

'At that time I was the only black teacher in all of London. Yes. I was quite a phenomenon.'

'Why didn't you quit and try another school?'

'Because I couldn't afford to quit. It was the first job I'd found after nearly sixteen months of search. It wasn't the job I wanted, but at least it relieved me from exposure to the tiresome round of rejections.' (Braithwaite 1978: 44–5)

I shall never forget the effect on me of Soyinka's poem, 'Telephone Conversation' (1970), when I first read it in class at the age of fifteen. It was a similar response to the one I had felt four years earlier when my primary school teacher had read the story of the crucifixion, which included what seemed to me at the time to be a graphic description of the nailing of Christ's hands to the cross. I could not believe that anyone could be so cruel and inhumane. Similarly, the rejection of the caller in Soyinka's poem, on the basis of his skin tone, was unthinkable to me. The ironic retort of the male caller to the landlady's question 'ARE YOU LIGHT OR VERY DARK?' was a response that had been rehearsed by numerous attempts to find suitable accommodation.

These may have been anecdotal instances of racial prejudice but housing and employment statistics show that Black Britons, even today, are more likely to occupy lower quality housing and lower status jobs than White Britons are. Furthermore, whereas these writers were drawing our attention to racism in British society, we are today acutely aware that the problem is a pervasive and sometimes violent one. Even as I write the trial of the neo-nazi bomber, David Copeland, has just ended. Copeland, a member of the National Socialist Movement, was responsible for detonating bombs in Brixton Market, Brick Lane and Soho. The last bomb, in a Soho pub, killed several people. These were tragic events but for every one that hits the headlines there are hundreds more incidents of racial violence around the country that diminish the quality of life in multiracial Britain. Each one is a salutary reminder that we all share in the responsibility for social justice.

The politics of 'race'

Around the time that Braithwaite and Soyinka were writing of their experience, action in political spheres was premised upon covert opinion as a memorandum to the Cabinet meeting of 30th January 1954 implied:

It would obviously be impossible to discriminate openly against coloured people as such in administration or legislation in the field of employment. After thorough examination of the possibilities the committee have come to the conclusion that it is not practicable to take steps to prevent coloured people obtaining employment once they are in this country. Any action to that end would have to be directed to preventing them or discouraging them from entering the United Kingdom. (Sir David Maxwell Fyfe cited in Panayi 1999: 45)

Towards the end of the 1960s, around the time of the first wave of migration of East African Asians, mainly from the newly independent state of Kenya, the right-wing Conservative MP, Enoch Powell, did more than anyone to popularise resentment against black migrants, in a series of public speeches (Panayi 1999: 141). Since Powell, a succession of anti-immigration and racist speeches by politicians has intermittently fuelled racial tension in Britain. There emerged during this period a network of racist and neo-Nazi groups dedicated to racial violence and the repatriation of Black Britons. The extent to which these groups would go to achieve their aims is documented by organisations such as Searchlight and the ex-Nazi turned 'mole' Ray Hill (Hill and Bell 1988).

From the outset there was an ambivalent attitude to Black migration. On the one hand there was a grudging acceptance of those people who were already present, an acceptance born of economic necessity. But on the other, there was pressure to keep others out. No doubt if Britain's history had been different, the Government of the day would have treated migrants more as 'gast arbeiter' (guest workers), as the German Government did, than as British citizens with a right of entry and abode in the United Kingdom. Successive Immigration and Nationality Acts since the 1960s have done exactly what Fyfe's memorandum suggested in the 1950s. The legacy of this siege mentality is felt even to the present day. Shortly before this chapter was written, 58 young Chinese men and women were found suffocated while in transit, in a container lorry at Dover. For non-white people especially, contrary to what those on the far right of British politics would have us believe, migration to Britain has never been an easy business. If it were, desperate people would not need to risk life and limb to gain entry.

Education policy and practice: assimilate and integrate!

Like housing and employment, early education provision for minority ethnic pupils was equally symptomatic of social and political attitudes. However, in addition to 'race', educational provision was also problematised around issues of language and culture, which led to a new variant of racism.

In educational policy, the preoccupation during the 1960s was on absorbing migrant children into British society. Multicultural and anti-racist educationalists have dubbed this period the 'assimilationist phase' and trace persistent and damaging stereotypes back to this period of educational and social policy (Cohen and Cohen 1986). In a critique of assimilationism the Inner London Education Authority (ILEA 1983b) identified the following major beliefs underpinning the approach:

- race relations in Britain were mainly good and any problems were caused by right-wing groups;
- the curriculum should reflect British traditions, history, customs and culture;
- all children were the same and difference should be ignored;
- the priority for black people must be learning to speak and write correct English before anything else can be learned.

(ILEA 1983b: 5)

Rapid acquisition of English then was central to educational concerns, as a Government circular at the time indicated: 'From the beginning the major educational task is the teaching of English.' (DES Circular 7/65, cited in Swann 1985:192). Swann (1985) noted that at that time, because the acquisition of English was perceived to be the 'problem', children from the Caribbean were deemed to have no particular educational need. However, seven years later the DES was recommending LEAs to deal sensitively with the under-achievement of 'West Indian' children by providing specialist English teaching. In the same document the department expressed concern at the 'disproportionate number of West Indian Children in ESN schools and classes in Greater London.' In 1972 4.9 per cent of pupils in ESN schools were of Black Caribbean heritage whereas they made up 1.1 per cent of the pupil population generally (Tomlinson 1983). Bernard Coard (1971) found that a significant number of Black Caribbean pupils were wrongly categorised as ESN and that once placed in special schools were given a restricted curriculum and teaching approaches, which failed to offer sufficient intellectual stimulation, leading to the construction of those pupils as educational failures.

After repeated expressions of concern on this issue, the Government set up an inquiry in 1979 to investigate the needs of children from all ethnic groups with a particular focus on children of 'West Indian' origin. The Inquiry team's interim report confirmed that urgent action was required to improve the educational achievement of African Caribbean pupils but rejected the language deficit argument. Although it found no single cause for underachievement, it cited a range of causal factors with the major ones being racism, negative teacher attitudes, an ethnocentric curriculum and examination system, poor nursery provision and ineffective school to home partnerships (Rampton 1981: 70–71).

More recently, a review of ten studies concludes that negative teacher attitudes cause unfavourable treatment of pupils of Caribbean heritage and that Black pupils respond by either accommodating or resisting the stereotypes teachers have of them (Nehaul 1996). Irrespective of the individual pupil's response, conclusions drawn from these studies suggest that the combined effect of teacher attitudes and institutional practices generally hinder the academic progress of many African-Caribbean heritage pupils. Findings from systematic monitoring in one LEA show an alarming deterioration in the attainment of African Caribbean pupils during their schooling. From a position of high attainment in baseline assessments African Caribbean pupils were found to be some 41 percentage points below their starting point by the time they reached GCSE (Gillborn and Mirza 2000: 6).

A year after the 1965 circular Central Government made additional funding available to those Local Authorities where there was a need to: '. . . make special provision in the exercise of any of their functions in consequence of the presence within their areas of substantial numbers of immigrants from the Commonwealth whose language or customs differ from those of the community . . .' (Section 11 of the Local Government Act 1966).

With effect from 1967 Local Authorities were able to claim 50 per cent of salary costs from the Home Office. Two years later the grant was increased to 75 per cent of costs at local level and remained constant until 1992. The combined effect of Circular 7/65 and Section 11 sent clear signals to Local Authorities about where the money should be channelled. Of all local government functions it was education that attracted the lion's share. LEAs largely used the grant to employ teachers to teach 'immigrant' children English. Throughout its life more Section 11 money was targeted towards the needs of pupils for whom English was an additional language than the needs of African-Caribbean pupils; a fact that drew strong criticism from the Black-British community. Towards the demise of Section 11, Local Education Authorities attracted 97 per cent of all available Section 11 grant. By this time, however, a significant proportion of minority ethnic pupils were born in Britain and the focus had widened to raising educational achievement, with English as an Additional Language (EAL) subsumed to that purpose.

During the 1980s, criticism of Section 11 came from official sources as well as the Black community. Recognising it as a valuable source of funding, Rampton nevertheless identified several drawbacks with Section 11. Firstly, it failed to meet the needs of a sufficiently wide range of minority ethnic groups and excluded second and subsequent generations of Commonwealth heritage people from the benefits of the grant. Secondly, responses to the needs of minority ethnic communities in some areas were far from comprehensive and lacked coordination. Thirdly, in other areas there was political opposition to finding the 25 per cent funding necessary to attract the Home Office allocation. Once money had been allocated Local Authorities were not obliged to identify staff employed under Section 11 and there was no requirement on them to monitor their effectiveness (Rampton 1981: 68–69). Changes to Section 11 occurred slowly during the first two decades of its life. Only after an HMI inspection in 1986/7 when the practise of using Section 11 money to fund mainstream posts was found to be widespread was action taken. The Home Office made the identification of Section 11 staff obligatory. However, it took the Local Government (Amendment) Act of 1993 to extend Section 11 provision to all minority ethnic groups.

From 1966 until the mid 1980s received wisdom dictated that the acquisition of English should be done in withdrawal classes or units. Some of these units were not only poorly equipped but were staffed by teachers grounded in a dubious pedagogy. The authority I worked in at the time closed its 'Language Units' in 1986, on advice from HMI. In their place the Authority created multicultural resource centres, each with a coordinator charged with developing multicultural education in local schools. This was not quite the paradigmatic shift it appears because job descriptions also included the teaching of English as a second language. Nevertheless, it did represent a new climate of opinion following the publication of *Education for All* (Swann 1985). Shortly before the closure of the 'units' I was able to visit one. It consisted of two classrooms, one for boys, the other for girls. The class of boys, ranging from Key Stage 1 to Key Stage 4, sat at desks that had been discarded from 'mainstream' schools. The books they read were dated and worn. I witnessed a lesson in which the boys, seated at their desks in rows, took turns to read aloud to the rest of the class from a class 'reader'.

In other Authorities the situation was worse and involved the bussing of hundreds of minority ethnic pupils to schools outside their local community. The practice of dispersal stemmed from political fears at the time, which were evident in a speech to the House of Commons by the Minister for Education in 1963: 'If possible, it is desirable on education grounds that no one school should have more than about 30 per cent of immigrants . . .' (cited in Swann 1985: 193). Circular 7/65, entitled 'Spreading the Children' gave the green light to LEAs to put political rhetoric into practice:

> Experience suggests, however, that . . . up to a fifth of immigrant children in any group fit in with reasonable ease, but that, if the proportion goes over about one third either in the school as a whole or in any one class, serious strains arise. It is therefore desirable that the catchment areas of schools should, wherever possible, be arranged to avoid undue concentrations of immigrant children. Where this

proves impracticable simply because the school serves an area which is occupied largely by immigrants, every effort should be made to disperse immigrant children round a greater number of schools . . .

(cited in Swann 1985: 194).

In some LEAs the practice of 'bussing' continued well into the 1980s until finally challenged by the Commission for Racial Equality in a test case. The subsequent report by the CRE (1986), following its investigation of admissions policy to schools in Calderdale, found that the authority had indirectly discriminated against Asian pupils. In order to gain admission to its mainstream schools pupils had to pass a test in English. Those who failed were allocated places in separate language units. Many of the units in areas of the authority populated by Asian communities were full with the result that approximately 49 per cent of Asian pupils who required EAL support were bussed to units outside their community. Many of these children (74 per cent) were infants who had to endure long bus journeys. Some of them missed parts of their schooling because the bus dropped them at school after the start of lessons. The Commission also found that the Authority's policy and practice disadvantaged Asian pupils and their parents by denying them rights of appeal that applied to parents of children attending mainstream schools. The curriculum adopted by these language units was found to be less extensive than the mainstream schools' curriculum and pupils' language development was hindered by the absence of 'native speakers of English'. The principle of curriculum entitlement for all, which has been central to the National Curriculum since The Education Reform Act of 1988, marked an important step towards equality of educational opportunity, at least in terms of access to a common curriculum.

The 1960s then, was characterised by official policy and practice based on the assumed 'deficiencies' of migrant children and the need to limit their presence in classrooms and schools. The late 1960s and early 1970s produced a variant of assimilationism and a step on the continuum towards multiculturalism. What became known as the integrationist phase continued the notion that Britain was a monocultural society into which the new migrants should be absorbed but it began to challenge the notion that problems would dissolve once migrant children had acquired English. While retaining an emphasis on the need to change the language and culture of migrants, proponents of an integrationist approach suggested that an understanding of minority ethnic group cultures was needed in order to appreciate the difficulties faced by migrants who were in the process of adapting to life in Britain (Bolton 1979 cited in Swann 1985: 196).

Throughout the 1970s there was growing recognition that assimilationist and integrationist approaches were not appropriate to the needs of an increasingly diverse multicultural society. This realisation was partly prompted by British born Black and Asian young people who asserted their right to maintain their languages, cultures and religions (Cohen and Cohen 1986). Linguistic and cultural maintenance is one means by which Black and Asian individuals and groups retained their dignity in the face of racial hostility, as the following quotations testify:

> When people came here . . . to survive . . . many people felt they had to become modern i.e. adopt British habits of food, clothes etc. They did this and then learned they were not being accepted. They had made a sacrifice for nothing and then they came back to their culture because it is more fulfilling. (Harpinder)

> When we first came to England in 1966, I thought Panjabi would die out because we had no contact with other Panjabis . . . People on arrival believed that everything in Britain would be okay. Then they realised because of poor housing, working conditions and racism . . . we cannot fit with society. They (white people) won't let us fit. We now get more comfort from mixing with our own community. (Taljeet)

> (Gardner 1987)

Education policy and practice: multicultural and anti-racist perspectives

A generation had faced the kind of racial prejudice reflected in the writings of Braithwaite and Soyinka, among others. They were growing up at a time when racial politics and political change generally was being played out on the international stage. In The United States during the late 1960s the Black Civil Rights Movement challenged white racism and feminism became more radical. The Sharpeville massacre in South Africa drew international attention to Apartheid and the struggle against it of the African National Congress (Mandela 1994: 225). By means of political osmosis across the globe and self-advocacy here, Black activism came to Britain.

Through its own networks the Black community challenged both the racism of the state and the prejudice of the streets by educating its young people (Sivanandan 2000). It also had other battles to fight with the re-emergence into the public arena during the 1970s of neo-Nazi organisations, culminating in the 1979 General Election campaign when the National Front held provocative marches and meetings in areas populated by Black Britons. This period brought an awareness of the racism of the streets as Sivanandan calls it, to the attention of white anti-racists who joined the struggle against racism and fascism. In terms of social advance the Race Relations Act 1976 was passed, making it unlawful for racial discrimination to occur either by intention or indirectly.

Within education there were parallel developments in policy and practice but there were also pedagogical, curricular and political schisms. One development took the line of 'cultural pluralism' (Cohen and Cohen 1986) or multiculturalism. The other sought to challenge the socio-cultural basis of racism and the structures that upheld it, through an anti-racist approach to education.

In its simplest form multicultural education incorporated an awareness of the music, clothes, food and festivals of minority ethnic groups into the curriculum. These initiatives were supported by the Government, which saw 'an appreciation of the cultural traditions of the countries of emigration' along with the development of 'rational attitudes to race and colour' as essential elements in the promotion of racial harmony (DES 1974). This approach was later criticised for several reasons. Firstly it was premised on a narrow view of culture, which had the effect of re-constructing, rather than deconstructing, racial stereotypes. A view of culture as spectacle and performance merely casts Black people as good dancers and artists (Jones 2000). Secondly, it tended to be peripheral to the curriculum and therefore had less status. A more enlightened approach to multicultural education integrated different cultural experiences within curricular themes with which all children could identify (Jeffcoate 1979: 34). In practice, however, multicultural education tended to be excluded from high status subjects such as literacy, mathematics and science (ILEA 1983b: 6), although gradually publications began to inform teachers of the potential of these subjects for a multicultural and anti-racist approach (Gill and Levidow 1987; ILEA 1985). Thirdly, it was premised upon the belief that if different 'cultures' were 'understood' prejudice would be eradicated. It therefore failed to recognise and take account of the historical and structural roots of racism and was considered irrelevant and superficial by some Black academics (Mullard 1984).

Some LEAs sought to synthesise the multicultural and anti-racist paradigms. In a policy commitment to racial equality ILEA (1983b: 6–7) incorporated features of multiculturalism within an anti-racist perspective. It recognised the need to value cultural identity and linguistic diversity but extended this to educational approaches that:

- gave voice to people's experience of racism and enabled black people greater influence over decisions;
- enabled all pupils and staff to identify and resist racism;
- were anti-discriminatory;
- raised teachers' expectations of pupils;
- included a curriculum that gave validity to the contribution of Black people to Britain and to the development of world knowledge.

These themes, in one form or another, have since been replicated in Government and quasi-governmental reports (see Chapter Three). The document was among the first to mention institutional racism, which it defined as a 'web of discrim-inatory policies, practices and procedures.' It also recognised the dehumanising effect of racism on both Black and White people. Adopting a similar position to ILEA, Grinter (1985) coined the term anti-racist multiculturalism to argue that anti-racist approaches and multicultural education were essential elements of a single perspective. Concurrent with the ILEA document was the publication of advice about the nature and scope of curriculum development for a multicultural society. From the late 1970s through to the 1990s there were variants of multi-culturalism being discussed around the country. The different versions were often dependent upon dominant political opinion at local level with the result that there was no agreed definition of multicultural education (Rex, in Swann 1985).

The move towards multiculturalism in its various guises influenced the work of Section 11 teachers and language assistants. Rampton (1981: 69) had proposed that Section 11 should be used to 'prepare all pupils for life in a multiracial society' as well as meet the specific needs of minority ethnic communities. By the mid 1980s it was widely accepted that Britain was and would continue to be a multi-cultural society. Perhaps the most influential publication to cement this reality in the mind of the educational world was the 'Swann Report'. Swann had taken over where Rampton had left off and had re-emphasised the need for education to be more responsive to a 'pluralist' society and that multicultural understanding should permeate the work of all schools and all aspects of each school's work. In a set of proposals to advance multicultural education by means of practical intiatives some of Swann's suggestions included:

- treating cultural diversity as a central feature in a broad and balanced curriculum;
- the appointment in each LEA of an adviser for multicultural education who would be responsible for the development of a pluralist approach and countering racism;
- the development of materials designed to reflect a pluralist approach.

(Swann 1985: 364–365)

Mindful of the fact that none of Rampton's recommendations had been implemented by Government, there was good reason for Ann Dummet, the then Director of the Runnymede Trust, to be sceptical about the influence of Swann (Dummett 1985). However, between the publication of the Swann Report and the re-structuring of Section 11 in 1992, multicultural education went through what might be described as its golden period. Certainly for those working in the field it was a time of optimism and vibrant activity.

My personal memories are testimony to this. I took up a Section 11 funded post in 1987 as an Area Coordinator for Multicultural Education. In addition to teaching English as a Second Language and coordinating a small team of language teachers and assistants, the post entailed the development of multicultural education in all the Area's schools through In Service Training (INSET) and the establishment and development of a multicultural resource centre. For the next five years there were a number of exciting initiatives, including the Linguistic Diversity in the Primary School Project; various DES funded courses, including the management of change for multi-ethnic schools and Education Support Grant funded posts in multicultural education. Practitioners created networks to disseminate materials and share good practice at conferences and events such as the annual Multicultural Swapshop. My work took me into dozens of schools where I was able to deliver INSET on bilingualism and linguistic diversity, multicultural and anti-racist education. I was able to assist head teachers to work with their staff to develop their multicultural curriculum. At the centre, colleagues worked assiduously to produce materials of quality to support developments in schools.

This impetus was initially slowed by the implementation of the National Curriculum. Despite reference to a 'broad and balanced' curriculum in which themes and dimensions such as multicultural education should permeate the core and foundation subjects and in spite of the eventual publication of cross-curricular guidance, the opportunity to create an 'education for all' with a truly multicultural perspective was squandered. The sheer pace of change and the fact that cross-curricular guidance was non-statutory oriented teachers' attention to those parts of the curriculum that were obligatory. The call upon Multicultural Education Services for INSET began to diminish and the number of teachers coming to borrow resources from our centre dwindled. Our response was to take resources to the schools. In any one term we were able to set up displays of resources linked to curriculum themes in 70 per cent of the Area's schools. We anticipated this would be an interim measure while the dust settled on the new curriculum and teachers once again felt the creative energy to make the content of their teaching less ethnocentric.

The Swann Report may have been the catalyst that multicultural education needed in the conservative shire counties, but as Gundara (2000) acknowledges, its roots, particularly with an anti-racist dimension, can be traced to the work of the Inner London Education Authority. Between 1975 and its abolition by the Conservative Government ten years later, ILEA produced a series of policy documents and aide memoires (ILEA 1981; 1983a, 1983b 1983c). Through its work, the Authority made a significant and widespread contribution to the intellectual debate around the theory and practice of education in a multi-ethnic society.

The real demise of multicultural and anti-racist education, or the threat of it, came with the Home Office's scrutiny of Section 11. The subsequent report had several positive recommendations. Through an expressed commitment to equality of opportunity it recommended that LEAs should set targets to raise the achieve-ment of minority ethnic children in their schools. This meant LEAs had to identify groups of pupils in need of support; demonstrate how they were to be supported, and report annually on their progress. However, it also recommended that the use of Section 11 grant to further the advance of multicultural education and the teaching of community languages should cease. This signalled the return of Section 11 to its assimilationist past, with an emphasis on EAL (English as an Additional Language) teaching. When the proposals were implemented in April 1992 the sepa-ration of a multicultural perspective from the work of Section 11 teachers meant that attempts to construct a coordinated approach to multicultural education withered on the vine.

From a personal perspective I felt that the change straitjacketed my work, restricted my creativity and undermined my values and principles. The manage-ment of change, at both national and local level, had been clumsy. It led to a great deal of stress among staff who received redundancy notices and had forced upon them the ignominy of having to re-apply for their own jobs. The fallibility of one's conditions of service as a Section 11 teacher was brought into a sharp focus by the short-term nature of new funding arrangements. Grants were allocated to projects with a 'shelf-life' of either three or five years and it became clear that a future 'career' as a Section 11 teacher carried with it the prospect of being shown the 'yellow card' every time a fresh bid was made for continued funding. These changes combined with a total disregard for one's professionalism, caused morale in the Service to plummet to the pit of depression. If equality of opportunity for the nation's minority ethnic children was the real purpose of Government policy, seriously lowering the morale of staff specifically funded to realise that aim was not the most intelligent way of achieving it.

In subsequent years several structural changes were made to Section 11. In 1995 a proportion of Section 11 money was diverted from the Home Office to Single Regeneration Budgets, designed to revitalise metropolitan areas. The next most significant change occurred in April 2000 after the education element of Section 11 was transferred to the DfEE. The grant was incorporated into the Standards Fund and finally renamed the Ethnic Minority and Travellers Achievement Grant (EMTAG). In line with a trend begun by the Local Management of Schools (LMS), EMTAG was devolved directly to those schools with significant numbers of minority ethnic pupils who were underachieving, relative to their majority ethnic peers. The intention was to integrate strategies to raise the achievement of minority ethnic pupils with whole-school approaches by enabling schools to appoint their own staff (DfEE 1998a). However, schools were given the option of 'buying back' to LEA provision. Local Education Authorities were given a strategic role through the appointment of advisory staff and the development of action plans based on specific outcomes. The Government re-stated both its commitment to equal opportunities and to EAL pupils, as well as those minority ethnic pupils 'at risk of under-achieving' (DfEE 1999a). The specific objectives of EMTAG were set out in Circular 16/99 as follows:

- to raise standards of achievement for those minority ethnic groups who are particularly at risk of under-achieving;
- to meet the particular needs of pupils for whom English is an additional language (EAL);
- to secure improved access to education, more regular school attendance and higher levels of attainment for Traveller children; and
- to meet the particular needs of refugee children.

(DfEE 1999b: B17.1)

In order to meet these objectives the main functions of the grant were:

- to appoint teachers, classroom assistants (including bilingual staff) and nursery nurses to give EAL support, undertake home school liaison and to raise achievement in particular of African Caribbean, Gypsy Traveller and refugee pupils;
- to cover the costs of relevant continuing professional development of EMTAG and 'mainstream' staff;
- to enable the purchase of teaching materials appropriate to the particular needs of EAL pupils and those at risk of underachievement.

(DfEE 1996: B17.3)

In return for financial provision schools were asked to undertake a range of measures to ensure that levels of attainment were raised. These included: the effective deployment of EMTAG staff; monitoring achievement and target setting, and appropriate continuing professional development to increase teachers' expertise in meeting the particular needs of minority ethnic pupils. The latter included specific reference to training in the National Literacy Strategy (NLS) for EAL teachers. In the first year of the 'new' fund particular emphasis was given to 'effective approaches to support Black-Caribbean children in the transition from Key Stages 2 to 3; EAL teaching at Key Stage 1 and the improvement of attainment of Traveller pupils at Key Stages 3 and 4 (DfEE 1999b: B17.9). LEAs were charged with the task of monitoring the effectiveness of provision and supporting schools to achieve their targets by means of the dissemination of good practice.

The underlying intention was not only to make education more accessible to those minority ethnic groups that had been identified as under-achieving but also to move towards greater equality of educational outcome across all ethnic groups.

However, the emphasis on EAL and NLS in the absence of a broader 'anti-racist multicultural' perspective appears to place EMTAG closer on the continuum to assimilationism than an inclusive approach for social justice.

As was the case with Section 11, the particular approach adopted in schools and LEAs is likely to be influenced by attitudes and perspectives at local level, including the intentions of head teachers. In turn these may be informed by the findings and recommendations of a series of reports that have appeared since 1996, which feature in Chapter Two. What is clear, and it has been the case for the last thirty years, is that there is a lack of consensus about what makes good educational practice in multicultural classrooms.

Summary

Since the 1960s Britain has developed diverse and conflicting approaches to education for its multi-ethnic society. Initially, provision for migrant pupils, mostly of South Asian origin, sought to assimilate them into British society through programmes of English language teaching. Teaching was often conducted in withdrawal classes and units, which created a form of educational apartheid.

This approach was succeeded by an integrationist model, which took account of the need to understand where migrant children were 'coming from'. Knowledge of homelands and aspects of culture developed into various forms of multiculturalism as the number of minority ethnic pupils who were British born increased. Some forms of multicultural education were nothing more than 'add-ons' to the curriculum and took the form of the occasional celebration of a religious festival, such as Diwali. Other forms sought to integrate the multicultural reality of modern Britain into broad curriculum themes and topics. Multicultural approaches were criticised for their tokenism by anti-racist educators, who argued that institutionalised racism needed to be eradicated in order to create a multicultural society premised upon social justice and equality.

Some writers on the subject refer to the different approaches as phases in a continuum from assimilationist to anti-racist education and although it is useful to present the different forms in some kind of chronology, the picture is much more complex than this model suggests. Allied to each approach is a particular political ideology; a particular view of the child and his or her needs and a particular perspective of society. The different forms that 'multicultural education' took have been dependent upon political opinion and pressure at local, as well as national level. In some LEAs, therefore, assimilationist tendencies were still in existence when others had dispensed with them, preferring more enlightened forms. Indeed, it is highly likely that the reason why there is no national consensus about the exact form education for a diverse multicultural society should take, is that myriad versions exist around the country, each situated in localised political ideology and opinion. What might be considered appropriate in the metropolitan boroughs might be thought too sensitive in some shire counties, even where issues are similar. However, the 1988 Education Reform Act created a national approach to education. Other nationwide initiatives in literacy and numeracy have followed, consolidating a more collective perspective in education. A clearer view of what it means to live in a diverse post-modern multicultural society will inform what needs to be done in education.

CHAPTER 2

The curriculum: breadth and balance for all?

The National Curriculum was preceded by a detailed and thorough inquiry into the nature of an appropriate education for an ethnically diverse society (Swann 1985). Despite the criticism levelled at the 'Swann Report' for failing to advocate a stronger line on anti-racist education, it recognised the *ad hoc* nature that multi-culturalism had taken across the country and recommended a more consistent national approach for all children in all schools, not just those in the cities and towns where ethnically diverse communities already existed. Rejecting the term 'multicultural education' in preference for 'Education For All' and promoting the concept of education for a pluralist society, the report was unequivocal about the need for a fundamental change to the curriculum. Swann stated that all children needed an understanding of Britain as a multiracial and multicultural society and that schools needed to combat the racism, inherited myths and stereotypes that were embedded in institutional practices. Perhaps the essence of Swann's perspective is encapsulated in the following statement:

> We believe it is essential to change fundamentally the terms of the debate about the educational response of today's multi-racial society and to look ahead to educating all children, from whatever ethnic group, to an understanding of the shared values of our society as a whole as well as to an appreciation of the diversity of lifestyles and cultural, religious, linguistic backgrounds which make up this society and the wider world. In so doing, all pupils should be given the knowledge and skills needed not only to contribute positively to shaping the future nature of British society but also to determine their own individual identities, free from preconceived or imposed stereotypes of their 'place' in that society.
>
> (Swann 1985: 316–317)

We might question what the 'shared values of our society' are and who decides what is a core value. We might want clarification of what 'an appreciation of the diversity of lifestyles and cultural, religious, linguistic backgrounds which make up our society and the wider world' actually means in practical terms, but the essential point about Swann is that a national approach for a culturally diverse society was being advocated. Concurrent with Swann was the debate about the construction of the National Curriculum. When the Statutory Orders were published there were traces of Swann's influence, but there was nothing very substantial to ensure the new curriculum would be permeated by a set of shared values and understandings of our pluralist society or how differences of power have structured inequality along the fault lines of 'race,' ethnicity, gender and class. If anti-racist educators considered Swann's recommendations mild, the National Curriculum was a sanitised version of Swann. However, appearance can sometimes obfuscate reality.

In the first half of this chapter there are two illustrations, based on the educational experience of students at De Montfort University, that are indicative of the extent to which the curriculum became consistently more multicultural in the period following Swann and the implementation of the National Curriculum. The second half of the chapter considers what future direction an anti-racist multicultural curriculum might take.

Testing the multicultural curriculum

In my lectures on 'Race' in Education to primary BEd and PGCE students at De Montfort University, I include a short quiz. It consists of a few simple questions that test students' knowledge of the history of Black and Asian Britain. The questions are as follows:

1. When did Black people first come to Britain?
2. Who made the first repatriation speech with reference to the Black presence in Britain?
3. How many Indian men fought as British soldiers during the First World War?
4. What do Florence Nightingale and Mary Seacole not have in common?

Like all quizzes and tests of 'general knowledge', these questions have an in-built cultural bias. Unlike most tests, this one, quite obviously, does not have a white anglocentric orientation. Nevertheless, most students, mature students apart, were between the ages of 10 and 12 when the National Curriculum was first introduced in 1988. It is a curriculum that has as a guiding principle breadth and balance and seeks to promote, amongst other things, the 'cultural development of pupils . . .' (DES 1989: 2). Furthermore, the History Programme of Study stated as one of its 'Key Elements' that pupils should be taught:

about the characteristic features of particular periods and societies, including the ideas, beliefs and attitudes of people in the past, and the experiences of men and women; and about the social, *cultural, religious and ethnic diversity of the societies studied*; (my italics)

(DFE 1995: 77)

The revised version of the Programme of Study in Curriculum 2000 was even more specific and referred to pupils being taught about: 'the social, cultural, religious and ethnic diversity of the societies studied, in Britain and the wider world . . .' (DfEE/QCA 1999a & b: 105)

Given the intended multicultural dimension to the National Curriculum, students who had experience of it as pupils ought to have been able to answer, if not all the questions, certainly some of them. However, the outcome on each occasion I have given the quiz has suggested that between the idea of the multicultural curriculum and its implementation in the classroom, there has been an information gap. The correct answer to the first question, is that Black people first came to Britain during the Roman occupation (Fryer 1984: 1). Only two students out of some 600 who have attended my lectures over the past three years have been able to give the correct answer. According to Fryer, it is documented that the first Black Roman soldier arrived in Britain around 210 AD and that a division of Black soldiers was stationed near Carlisle around 253 AD. No-one has known the answer to the second question, which is Queen Elizabeth I, who made the declaration on 11th July 1596 (Fryer 1984: 10). Equally, the third question has also remained unanswered. During the First World War an estimated 1.3 million Indian soldiers fought for Britain. Approximately 138,000 of them fought in the trenches, while others fought at Gallipoli, Mesopotamia, the Middle East and East Africa. In addition, Indian sailors served in the Merchant Navy (Visram 1995: 26). More students have been able to answer the final question but not in any great number. Like Florence Nightingale, Mary Seacole was a nurse who tended British troops in the Crimea. However, she differed in at least two respects. Firstly, she was Black. Secondly, she did not have Florence Nightingale's social connections. The latter was well connected to one of Buckinghamshire's landed families, the Verneys, while Mary came from more lowly origins in Jamaica. The authentic account of Mary Seacole's life is told in her autobiography entitled *The Wonderful Adventures of Mrs Seacole in Many Lands*, which was published in 1857 (Fryer 1984: 252).

In isolation, these questions appear to ask for arbitrary facts but, taken together, they represent a body of knowledge that is missing from the history of Britain taught in our schools. Why is the Black presence in Britain missing from the curriculum? The questions raise further questions about cultural representation. As a post-war child my televisual education largely consisted of grainy black and white war films. My staple reading consisted of comics with story lines centred on acts of bravery in front of enemy lines. Yet in all those years of watching and reading representations of the two World Wars, I cannot remember ever seeing a Black character. The response of my students to these questions suggests that a generation later nothing has changed. It is as though our history and cultural representations of it have been 'white-washed'. Black people, like women and working class people, are not part of the nation's official history. Their history has either been buried or else it is deemed inferior and not worthy of inclusion. Foucault (1980) calls this 'subjugated knowledge'; a concept I shall return to below.

Personal experiences of schooling

Given that there appeared to be a major discrepancy between one of the stated aims of the History curriculum and the actual diet my students had received, I was keen to explore in greater depth how pupils and students might have experienced the curriculum. To what extent had their schooling reflected their cultural heritage and how had education helped to shape their identities, if indeed it had? In order to make this enquiry, I interviewed a small sample of BEd undergraduate students. The sample consisted of three Sikh students, one Turkish-Cypriot and one Black-British student. All were female. Although the sample was small these students were able to share their experience of 13 different schools (8 primary and 5 secondary) covering a wide geographic area ranging from Inner London to the East and West Midlands. With the exception of two schools, all the schools were multi-ethnic. All five secondary schools had roughly even proportions of majority and minority ethnic pupils. Three primary schools had between 40 and 50 per cent minority ethnic pupils and two had between 16 and 20 per cent. These students left school between 1994 and 1995. This small study then, sought to investigate how these students had experienced education at multi-ethnic schools at a time when national policy encouraged 'breadth and balance' and sought to develop the cultures of all children.

I used a structured interview schedule, which included closed and relatively open-ended questions in order to elicit both factual and subjective answers to each student's experience of the curriculum and extra-curricular aspects of the schools they had attended.

Students' experience of maths and science

None of the students described the curriculum in any of the schools they had attended as a multicultural one. Two said the curriculum had been completely anglocentric, while the other three described it as mostly anglocentric. A closer breakdown of the curriculum into subjects showed that where a multicultural perspective was evident it tended to be restricted to particular subjects and to particular topics within subjects. Furthermore, these topics tended to be restricted to particular phases of education or even to a particular term in the educational year. None of the students reported evidence of a multicultural dimension in maths or science. We can infer from this that there was no explicit reference to scientific discoveries or mathematical developments emanating from non-European cultures or non-white thinkers. The subjects tended to be presented as decontextualised, neutral bodies of knowledge or were linked to advances made by European scientists and mathematicians. However, in mathematics all students engaged with algebra, which is an Arabic word. In addition, they understood negative numbers, which is made possible by the concept of zero, first introduced from Indian mathematics. By making reference to the origins of concepts, theories and discoveries, it is possible to locate mathematics and science in a global perspective. In doing so, it not only demonstrates that different cultures have contributed to world knowledge, but that the sharing of knowledge across cultures and between nations has been essential to human development throughout history.

English

Two students referred to the books of Black authors being read in English. But this was not until GCSE and the authors were well-known Black American writers such as Mildred D. Taylor (1977), Rosa Guy (1982) and Maya Angelou (1984). One student recalled being able to relate with implicit understanding to these writers. The depiction of family and the experience of racism resonated with her. The inclusion of world literature is important and clearly Black-American writers can strike personal chords with Black-British students. However, if our set books include only Black writers outside Britain then the type of multiculturalism being presented is one that is removed from our own society and reinforces the notion of multiculturalism as an 'outsider perspective'. The depiction of the Black-American experience of racism serves an important function in that it brings to the attention of white British pupils the injustices that have been perpetrated by White-European heritage people over Black-African heritage people. To consider the operation of racism at a distance from our immediate society might enable pupils to engage with the issue in a rational and dispassionate manner. However, if we deal only with injustice outside our own history and our own society, then the implicit message is that we, as a society, are either inherently good or else we are neutral. The truth is elsewhere and at some point there is a need to turn critical scrutiny on our own society. The inclusion of world class Black writers in the curriculum needs to be complemented by good Black-British writers and their white counterparts who depict life as it is in Britain today and in the past.

During the 1970s a British based 'multicultural literature' for young people began to emerge through the work of such writers as Farukh Dhondy (1976), Jan Needle (1979), Rukshana Smith (1982) and Marjorie Darke (1978). This development was reflected at Key Stage 1 but there was, and still is, a gap in the middle years. Twenty years on some of these texts appear dated and there is a continual need for new writers who are in tune with the current lived experience of young people and who are able to authentically reflect the diversity of human relations in the 'mirror' of literature. Meera Syal, the author of *Anita and Me* and *Life isn't all Ha Ha Hee Hee*, is probably our best current exemplar.

The body of British multicultural literature needs to be geared to readers across all age groups and abilities, not just those at GCSE level, or at Key Stage 1. It needs to cover the range of issues that apply to the human condition and not get 'tramlined' into the single issue of racism, important though this is. There is a need for a multicultural literature that deals with the ways individual identities and relationships are constructed and mediated at the intersections of cross-cultural influence and the various dimensions of gender, 'race', class, disability etc. The inclusion of an appropriate multicultural literature is as much the responsibility of publishers as it is of writers and teachers.

Students' experience of the foundation curriculum

RE

There was an equally uneven presence of multicultural education in foundation subjects and Religious Education across all key stages. Three of the five students described the RE curriculum as Christian and of the two who had experienced a multi-faith approach, one reported that this was at secondary school only and the other recalled a topic on world religions, which lasted for a term at middle school. Likewise, assemblies had been mainly Christian or secular with only occasional reference to their own or other non-Christian belief systems. Moral values are common to all faiths and it is possible to reflect this in schools. A glimpse of an inclusive approach to Religious Education was given recently by Inderjit Singh, the Editor of the *Sikh Messenger*. Speaking on Radio 4's Thought For the Day, he described a visit to the only Sikh school in the country. For that reason, one might have expected it to be a very conservative institution with a strict adherence to the teachings of the ten Gurus. In reality it was very different and in addition to evidence of Sikhism being taught (by a Muslim teacher), he saw children's work on the Jewish festival of Purim prominently displayed. The point is that one does not have to be a believer to teach about belief. Furthermore, a multi-faith approach enables pupils to see the essential similarities of faiths that to outward appearance seem dissimilar.

History and geography
There were few examples of a multicultural dimension in the humanities curriculum either. One student recalled a study of the Caribbean as a contrasting locality in geography and another reported that the geography of other countries did not extend beyond the study of maps and climate. Only one student could remember studying anything other than British history: a topic on the Aztec, Inca and Maya civilisations. The programmes of study for history at Key Stage 2 included a unit on a past non-European society with possible examples, including the Indus Valley, Mesopotamia and Benin (DFE 1995: 81). However, unless good quality materials are available, many teachers are unlikely to spend hours researching new areas of knowledge when there are commercially produced packs and books on Ancient Egypt. In consequence, the ancient histories of some of Britain's Black population remain obscure and unrecognised. More importantly, if young people are to have a good sense of their own history they need to be able to understand the significance of the present in the past. All too often the history of Britain is viewed through the lens of a particular 'white' experience. Class and gender usually circumscribe that particularity given that most writers of history have been men of privileged background.

Art and music
References to non-European artistic and musical traditions were equally tokenistic in the schools attended by these students. Again it was at upper or secondary school that multicultural elements were most apparent in the curriculum. One student had studied African and Islamic art at GCSE and a Sikh student had played in the school's steel band. A further issue emerged concerning the development of a multicultural curriculum. One student recalled how 'In middle and upper school when Indian music was used the examples tended to be bad ones, which made me cringe and children, both Asian and others, giggled.'

This example highlights the need for a sensitive approach to curriculum initiatives. As well as being mindful of the need to include aspects of various cultures in the curriculum, resources, artefacts and examples need to be selected judiciously. The use of a bad example can be counter-productive. One approach might be to start from current pop music and trace influences back to their cultural roots. There are exciting developments in the current music scene where cultural fusion is taking place. Alongside Blues and Jazz, with their roots in Africa via the USA, the strains of Latin American influence can be heard. Popular singers have incorporated musical traditions from around the world in their compositions and 'world music' now has a stage to play on in Britain through the initiative of Peter Gabriel and WOMAD. New forms are being developed by means of cross-cultural musical alliances. Asian Dub Foundation blends rap music with Bhangra to create a unique sound. These innovations are signs of the times and reflect the cultural transformations that are taking place across Britain and the world.

Curriculum, teaching and learning

A curriculum that incorporates these transformations is one that is able to contextualise current changes alongside older traditions and forms. For example, by demonstrating where influences in music originate, and by linking them to the past, young people may be better able to make connections across cultures and across time. The essential point is that effective teaching makes learning possible by placing new knowledge, skills and concepts in contexts that begin from the learner's current experience or frames of reference. By connecting with what is known the teacher can make learning both relevant and meaningful for the learner. It is at this point that curriculum, teaching and learning come together in a holistic process.

Education is fundamentally a social process. The construction of curricula and pedagogy is situated in social context. Knowledge is drawn from the physical and intellectual world. But the knowledge that is deemed important enough to be included in the curriculum has been mediated by the social world; it has had value placed upon it. People in superordinate positions who are themselves socially valued ascribe value. The curriculum, therefore, is a socially valued selection from all the knowledge that exists in the world. Within the curriculum, knowledge is categorised and hierarchically organised. In this way, some knowledge is subordinate to other knowledge. An example of this is the division between core and foundation subjects. Further hierarchies exist within superordinate knowledge. Currently, literacy is deemed more important than oracy, and within literacy metalinguistic knowledge is ascribed greater value than the creative application of language. This positioning of knowledge conveys important messages to teachers and learners in what might be described as an epistemological discourse. If teachers and learners discern that knowledge within the curriculum is valued differently, they will equally realise that knowledge that is left out of the curriculum is of lesser value than that which is included. If what is excluded is the knowledge that is most relevant to the learner, then not only is the potential of the teacher to create meaningful learning contexts reduced, but the affective response of the learner is likely to be positioned in opposition to the curriculum.

Classrooms are the interfaces where curriculum, teaching and learning meet and if learners perceive knowledge to have little relevance to their lives they are likely to become disassociated. That is, they will either resist the curriculum because it alienates them, or else respond compliantly by going through the motions of learning in order to meet alternative objectives. These might be extrinsic motives such as qualifications, or parental expectation. Learning, therefore, becomes a means to an end rather than a value in itself. Margaret Gibson (1988) found that ethnic groups who voluntarily migrate show a preparedness to accommodate the social practices of the dominant culture whilst simultaneously resisting assimilation. Academic success is, therefore, possible for certain minority ethnic groups within a system that pays little attention to their cultural identity. However, she asserts the onus for change should not fall on students but systems:

> By pressurising minority students to conform to majority social standards, with all the concomitants of racial prejudice, schools devalue those students' cultural traditions and contribute to an oppositional climate, a sense of 'us versus them' which can do much to undermine the instructional process. Minority students would accommodate themselves more readily to the formal demands of the school curriculum were their identities not challenged in the process . . . the concept of 'mainstream' . . . comprehends multiple cultural identities.
>
> (Gibson 1988: 200)

The experience of the students in my sample suggests the National Curriculum was a partial selection of knowledge, and one which was situated in a cultural frame that was, in the main, distinct from their own. It might be argued that the sample was small, unrepresentative and that generalisations cannot be made. However, equally significant is the point that this was a random sample of students, drawn from various locations, who had attended mainly multi-ethnic schools at a time in Britain's educational history when multicultural education was deemed to be an important dimension of the nation's curriculum approach. What these accounts demonstrate is how sparse the multicultural curriculum actually was in some of our multi-ethnic schools. Given that many 'all white' schools failed to even acknowledge the need to embrace multiculturalism on the grounds that they did not have minority ethnic children (Gaine 1988) we can begin to see the breadth of neglect. Furthermore, documentary analysis of the National Curriculum showed that while there was the gloss of a rhetorical commitment to equality issues, it remained a curriculum that was essentially monocultural, male centred and technocratic (Weiner 1994).

Several generations of young people, growing up in a multicultural society, were given adequate breadth and balance in their educational diet to enable them to take their place as adults in such a pluralist society. In contrast to their white counterparts, it is possible that minority ethnic students are better placed to understand the ramifications of plurality. As one of the students in my sample pointed out, this is in spite of what happens in school: 'My schooling had nothing to do with my culture. Schooling did not encourage our culture. We had a balance because we covered things outside school.'

Minority ethnic students have access to bi or multicultural experiences. Even those students who appear 'westernised' have the advantage of diverse frames of reference. Formal education schools them in one version of British culture but their informal education, that is the education they receive at home and in the community, not only gives them access to another version, but provides them with alternative modes of social action. Assimilationists had believed that exposure to two cultures would lead to 'culture shock' and psychological crisis. However, one student went on to say that school had helped her develop her sense of self because it enabled her to realise the difference between British culture and her own. Notwithstanding the point that British 'culture' is itself multifaceted, the student's sense of agency was emphatic when she made the point that it was she who chose, from the range of options available to her, what she wanted to be. A comment by another student shows how some schools can circumvent a prescriptive curriculum: 'Although the curriculum was anglocentric the ethos allowed pupils to share their cultural experiences'.

This point serves as a useful reminder that the curriculum can be defined in several ways and that in its broadest meaning it may refer to everything a school communicates to its members (Barnes 1976). A broad definition of curriculum would include the dominant attitudes and values communicated by school, as well as practices, procedures and behaviour legitimated by the institution's culture. However, even schools with a seemingly positive ethos can be partial in their acceptance of cultural experience. The same student also described how Asian pupils in the school were 'set apart' from their Black and White peers. Where the ethos of a school is ambiguous, marginalised individuals and groups are likely to feel that ambiguity in their personal response to school, as a third student demonstrated: 'There was an ambiguity. Inside I wanted to share my culture with everyone but outside I did not . . . It was only when I went to Turkish school that I felt more comfortable about my culture'.

The conflicts felt by minority ethnic pupils tends not to be because they reside in two or more cultures, but because the culture of home is subordinate to a dominant culture, which either renders them invisible, or else allows only partial glimpses of their 'other' selves by means of tokenistic displays. Only two students felt that their cultural backgrounds were understood at school and even then it was not until secondary school and involved a handful of teachers. All the students said that in the future the curriculum should be more multicultural. One student suggested that the presence and promotion of minority ethnic teachers who are able to bring their own authentic experience to bear on the curriculum would be an important development.

Given that these students were able to progress through a system that paid little regard to their cultural backgrounds, what was it that enabled them to achieve sufficiently to gain access to higher education? There appear to be two factors contributing to their success. One was teacher expectation; all five students recalled that teachers had good or high expectations of them. The other factor was encouragement to succeed by a significant other. In most cases this was a parent or parents but in a couple of cases it was an older sibling or a teacher, who took a special interest. Mentor schemes may, therefore, provide a useful substitute for young people who do not have a significant adult to encourage them.

Multicultural capital

Several students made the point that multicultural education is relevant to all pupils. Some said it was more important that majority ethnic pupils receive a comprehensive multicultural education than their minority ethnic counterparts. It could be argued that those least equipped with the necessary knowledge, skills and understanding to take their place as well educated adults in a multicultural society are indeed majority ethnic pupils. Whatever term is used to describe the curriculum, be it multicultural, anti-racist, pluralist, or the one that is currently in vogue, 'inclusive', what really matters is the form and content of that curriculum and its associated pedagogy.

In the second part of the chapter I want to outline some possibilities, but it is clear that such a curriculum needs to take account of the various forms of 'cultural capital' (Bourdieu and Passeron 1977) that exist in our society. By dealing with dominant forms of cultural capital, which in its simplest form is knowledge required in order to succeed academically, the needs of minority ethnic pupils and other marginalised groups might be addressed. The ability to accurately use Standard English, for example, is one facet of dominant cultural capital. Without it a pupil, of whatever background, is unlikely to succeed in academic terms. But our multicultural society has created other forms of cultural capital that need to be learned. These other forms include the customs, mores, values and codes of diverse cultures. A person who has 'multicultural capital' is someone who is able to decode and understand the diverse signs of their social and cultural world, someone who is comfortable residing in such a world and who is able to relate to that world with confidence. Such a person would neither feel that their own identity is threatened by difference, nor would they feel superior to those who appear different. A further feature of 'multicultural capital' is recognition that culture and identity are not fixed in time and space but continually change. Individuals are not one-dimensional and may be simultaneously affiliated to several cultures.

> Every individual may take part in a range of different cultures and communities. Some of these may be at variance with each other. Many are interrelated and continually exchanging with each other. All are in a state of development . . . Not all cultures and communities have equal status: the formation of personal identities may therefore take place within contexts of uneven power and influence.
>
> (The Runnymede Trust 1993)

A multicultural curriculum has to affirm individual and collective identities. It needs to take account of the inter-relatedness of cultures and the rights of individuals to make informed choices about cultural affiliation, while recognising that such choices are influenced by dynamic social forces. It needs to recognise how 'the uneven distribution of power' has positioned people differently and enable pupils to develop critical insights into how and why such differentials exist and how they might be challenged. From this discussion it follows that the multicultural curriculum is applicable to every classroom in every school in the country.

A curriculum for our times?

Since 1988 curriculum change has almost reached the status of permanent revolution. There have been five significant changes to the curriculum in little more than a decade. However, for the foreseeable future Curriculum 2000 (DfEE/QCA 1999a and b) will inform curriculum delivery. It seems fitting therefore to identify what the new curriculum might offer multicultural classrooms. Whereas the publication of the original National Curriculum was staggered, with cross-curricular guidance lagging behind the statutory elements, the new document incorporates cross-curricular dimensions in its introduction. By means of an articulation of values, aims, purposes and general teaching requirements the document espouses positive intentions. These immediately signal the possibility of a holistic curriculum along the lines suggested above. Since the document is so important to curriculum developers it might be useful to extrapolate pertinent references.

Values

Recognising the interrelationship of education and society, and the way social values are embedded in the educational process is useful.

> Education influences and reflects the values of society, and the kind of society we want to be. It is important, therefore, to recognise a broad set of common values and purposes that underpin the school curriculum and the work of schools
>
> (p.10)

An explicit statement of common values is made (pp.147–149) in terms of their meaning for the self, relationships, society and the environment. Self-understanding, self-respect and responsibility for self are complemented by such things as refusal to 'support values or actions that may be harmful to individuals or communities' (p.148). By implication, such negative values and actions must include racism and racial harassment. However, this statement of itself is not explicit enough to convey such an intention. An anti-racist interpretation is only likely to occur if the reader brings to the text a concern about racism and actively engages this perspective in the reading. However, under the framework for personal social and health education (PSHE) and citizenship, Key Stage 2 non-statutory guidance suggests that being an active citizen involves realising the consequences of bullying and racism on individuals and communities (p.139). Pupils need to be taught about the factors that create diversity and how to respond to racism, including how to seek help (p.140).

Aims, purposes and inclusion

Elsewhere, there are further statements to reinforce a positive, anti-discriminatory intent. The curriculum should, for example, 'enable pupils to challenge discrimination and stereotyping' (p.11).

Again, it is possible to read an anti-racist perspective into this generic statement, which, rightfully, must include gender, class and disability, as other key areas requiring active critical scrutiny. In the section of the document dealing with principles of inclusion this point is reiterated through examples of effective teaching environments. In addition to being ones in which all pupils feel secure and where their contributions to learning are valued, they are also ones in which pupils view difference positively, 'whether arising from race, gender, ability or disability' (p.31). The need for pupils to feel secure within school, both in physical terms and in terms of cultural identity, is exemplified with reference to challenging bullying and racial harassment and the acceptance of clothing appropriate to religious beliefs (p.32). It has long been known that the need to feel confident, secure and valued within the classroom is a prerequisite to becoming an effective, self-motivated and independent learner (Maslow 1976).

Within PSHE and citizenship education there is reference to the importance of developing individual and collective identity in relation to diverse cultures present in Britain and the wider world. PSHE is intended to be an integral part of the curriculum with the intention that it should develop pupils' knowledge and understanding of how beliefs and cultures influence individuals and societies (p.11). Furthermore, learning to 'respect our common humanity, diversity and differences . . .' is rightly regarded as essential to the development of 'effective, fulfilling relationships' in school and throughout life (p.136).

Clearly, there is an intention that a positive multicultural and anti-discriminatory strand should permeate the curriculum. The aims, values and purposes of the curriculum are supported by the framework for PSHE and citizenship education and equality of curriculum access for all pupils, including those for whom English is an additional language. (pp.33, 37). However, intentions are not always implemented. As is evident in the survey conducted with De Montfort students, the multicultural dimension, which should have permeated the curriculum following ERA was far from comprehensive.

The extent to which intentions might be more resilient in the new curriculum can perhaps be better predicted by scrutinising what is contained in the statutory aspects rather than the non-statutory sections of the document.

The core and foundation subjects

Across all key stages literature should include stories, poems and drama from a range of cultures (En2). At Key Stages 3 and 4 the study of literature is expected to include inter-cultural comparisons of texts. In addition, the study of language variation encompasses the ways in which English has changed over time and how it has been influenced by other languages (En1). Since the eclectic nature of English is reserved for the latter key stages, it must be assumed that this constitutes progression in the study of language variation which focuses on differences between Standard English and other dialect forms at Key Stage 2. It is noteworthy, however, that the document refers to 'standard and dialect forms', which suggests, erroneously, that 'standard' is not a dialect of English. It might be implied, therefore, that non-standard dialects of English are lesser forms or else are aberrations of the 'standard'. This implication, together with the absence of any recognition that English has borrowed words from other languages, may mean that the opportunity to reflect linguistic diversity in the English curriculum at Key Stages 1 and 2 is greatly reduced.

The introduction to mathematics in the new curriculum across all key stages is promising. In a bold and unequivocal statement we are told that: 'Different cultures have contributed to the development and application of Mathematics. Today the subject transcends cultural boundaries and its importance is universally recognised.' (DfEE/QCA 1999a: 60; DfEE/QCA 1999b: 57). Given that the programmes of study in mathematics make no reference to the cultures that have contributed to the subject, pupils are likely to receive a mathematics education that leaves them with the assumption that it is indeed a universal, culture neutral body of knowledge. At the very least, the subject's breadth of study ought to include reference to the cultural roots of different aspects of mathematics.

In a similar way the introduction to science states that: 'Pupils recognise the cultural significance of science and trace its worldwide development.' (DfEE/QCA 1999a: 76; DfEE/QCA 1999b: 102). However, such recognition is unlikely to happen unless it is explicitly taught and there is no reference to 'the cultural significance of science' in the programmes of study. At Key Stage 1 there is the possibility that physical characteristics of 'race' might emerge as pupils: 'recognise similarities and differences between themselves and others . . . (Sc2, 4a)

A curriculum that includes in its aims pupils who are able to challenge stereotypes and racism needs to make explicit the role of science in demystifying the physical aspects of difference. Learning about the reasons for varieties of skin tone is one example we expect to see in a science curriculum in a multiracial society. At Key Stages 3 and 4 we might expect an aspect of the study of human beings and of evolution to include genetic similarity across human groups and the debunking of pseudo-scientific racism.

Programmes of study in the core curriculum then, appear to offer little scope for the application of the intended curriculur aims, which include a positive multi-cultural and anti-racist perspective. What scope might be found in the foundation subjects?

The capacity for Information and Communication Technology (ICT) to enable pupils 'to access ideas and experiences from a wide range of people, communities and cultures' (DfEE/QCA 1999a: 96; DfEE/QCA 1999b: 143) is identified in the introduction to the subject. The use of email enables pupils to exchange information across the world; to ask questions and receive answers about the lives of children in other locations. Certainly the information revolution provides wider access to different cultures and alternative views of history. However, access alone does not guarantee all the people of the world an authentic voice. The power to control what might be accessed and the actual content of information might remain invested with the rich and powerful nations, or indeed rich and powerful companies of the world. There is also an assumption of universal access. Until all pupils in all schools in Britain have access to the Internet its power as a resource and communicative tool will not be realised. The same point might be made for all pupils in all schools throughout the world. Expensive technology can only be afforded by those with the means to purchase it and there is great disparity of means within our own society and throughout the world. Nevertheless, the Internet and digital televisual broadcasting have brought other languages and other cultures into our living rooms. Using the remote control for the digi-box, I can switch, within seconds, between a gritty British inner-city drama, and a Panjabi love song on the Lashkara channel. However, I am still waiting to see fully developed, authentic Black and Asian characters in British drama. Access alone cannot eradicate omission, contradiction and stereotype, but critical reflection, encompassing ethical and moral issues in connection with ICT, is reserved for Key Stage 4.

The need to reflect social, cultural, religious and ethnic diversity of societies at different historical periods is retained in the new curriculum document at Key Stages 2 and 3 (p.105). Several study units at Key Stage 2 offer clear opportunities for an exploration of multi-ethnic Britain. The study of local history (unit 7) can involve population movement, including the settlement in the area of people from different cultures (p.107). It might also include religious practices and the contributions of significant individuals. For teachers working in multi-ethnic communities this unit enables schemes of work that fully explore, by means of documentary evidence and oral histories, the history of their multicultural community. In some areas schools have combined a local study with 'Roots to the Future', a touring exhibition of significant Black-British people throughout history (CRE). Schools in areas lacking cultural diversity might look to unit 10, 'Britain and the wider world in Tudor times' for an opportunity to investigate how and why

London throughout the Tudor period became increasingly multi-ethnic. As well as considering settlers, there is scope to investigate the inter-relationship of Britain with Africa and Asia as trading partners. Such schools might also look at emigration and immigration as an aspect of Britain since 1930 (unit 11b) and the contribution of Mary Seacole (unit 11a – Victorian Britain).

Similar opportunities arise at Key Stage 3, which includes two world studies, a European study and three British studies. Examples of what might be covered include the influence of the Jews (Britain 1066–1500); the Plantations in Ireland (Britain 1500–1750); Empire and colonial rule in India and the abolition of the slave trade, including the role of Olaudah Equiano, the Black reformer (Britain 1750–1900) and the Crusades and Islam (European study before 1914). The content of a 'Study of the World before 1900' unit is explicitly multicultural since its core activities involve the investigation of 'the cultures, beliefs and achievements of an African, American, Asian or Australasian society' and the study of the world after 1900 includes references to Mahatma Gandhi and Martin Luther King, as well as the possibility of studying the rise of Fascism (DfEE/QCA 1999b: 150–53).

The intention to reflect cultural and ethnic diversity in history at Key Stage 2 is not explicitly supported by the Qualifications and Curriculum Authority's (QCA) schemes of work published on the Net. The one key historical figure referred to is Florence Nightingale. There is, however, one slight hint at the possibility of a multicultural dimension in the QCA work. The scheme on Britain since 1948 does refer to the study of changes caused by immigration and emigration, but this is only a possibility and is open to the discretion of individual schools and teachers.

Returning to Foucault's notion of 'subjugated knowledge' there are opportunities for teachers to construct a history curriculum capable of including such knowledge and in doing so of giving history a new frame of reference and a fresh way of interpreting the social relations of the present. Within our communities, irrespective of where they are located, there are diverse resources amongst marginalised groups waiting to be to be tapped. Stories and oral histories, songs and music, beliefs and worldviews can be made integral to the curriculum rather than left as appendages to it. Kincheloe and Steinberg (1997) propose a critical multiculturalism, which starts from the premise that the histories of marginalised groups *is* subjugated knowledge and that a truly inclusive curriculum must incorporate subjugated perspectives.

The programmes of study for Geography begin:

As pupils study Geography, they encounter different societies and cultures. This helps them realise how nations rely on each other. It can inspire them to think about their own place in the world, their values, and their rights and responsibilities to other people and the environment.

Curriculum content in Geography across all key stages does provide opportunities to study: other locations; the interrelationship of people and places across the world and the reciprocal influence of people and environment. At Key Stage 2 the proactive capacity of people in a variety of locations to improve their environment is considered alongside political influences in the sense of how decisions might affect people's lives (p.113). In a variety of ways these themes are extended at Key Stage 3 and include such issues as the interrelationship of population and resources (p.158) and differences in development within as well as between countries (p.159). There is scope here to increase pupils' understanding of the ways in which wealth and power have and do change people's relationship to their environment.

Learning a modern foreign language (MFL) is not a statutory requirement until Key Stage 3. However, many primary schools do teach a MFL, some as early as Year 4. The inclusion of curriculum guidance is, therefore, useful particularly since learning an additional language 'raises awareness of the multilingual and multi-cultural world' and enables cross-cultural comparisons to be made (p.142). Bilingual pupils are likely to be at an advantage when learning a new language because they already posses a metacognitive view of language and recognise its arbitrary nature. However, they are likely to be disadvantaged if they want to study their first language to exam level because schools must offer official working languages of the European Union before other languages, even ones spoken by thousands of people within an EU country. When selecting their language option, bilingual speakers are likely to have to choose between an EU language or their own, or else study one of them in a 'twilight' class. This demarcation between EU languages and non-EU languages reinforces the language hierarchy, which subordinates Asian languages to European ones, thereby perpetuating implicit racism.

The Art and Design curriculum offers pupils the opportunity to study the 'diverse roles and functions of art, craft and design in contemporary life, and in different times and cultures (p.116), which at Key Stage 1 involves looking at the similarities and differences in the works of art and craft. At Key Stage 2 progression in this multicultural dimension involves pupils looking at the roles and purposes of artists, designers and craftspeople at different times and from different cultures. This is further developed at Key Stage 3 with the consideration of the genres, styles and traditions in art, craft and design in different social and cultural contexts (p.169).

Breadth of study in Music at all key stages requires pupils to be taught knowledge, skills and understanding through a range of music including live and recorded music from different times and cultures. In addition, selecting and combining musical structures, genres, styles and traditions can enhance composition skills.

Overview

This brief documentary analysis suggests some potential for a multicultural curriculum to be constructed at the level of individual schools. However, it should be remembered that the National Curriculum provides 'baseline' curriculum entitlement for children across the country. Simply because an explicit, comprehensive multicultural dimension is not there does not mean it cannot be taught. The above examples may make obvious reference to the multicultural dimension but teachers who bring a knowledge and understanding of what such a dimension involves will read additional possibilities into the rubric. Those teachers who have a multicultural and anti-racist perspective will apply that perspective to their teaching in the full knowledge that they are meeting the underlying principles of the stated curriculum aims. However, the evidence to date suggests this is not a common attribute among teachers and that provision is currently 'patchy' and likely to remain so.

The development of a comprehensive multicultural dimension to the curriculum is problematic for several reasons. Although there is clear intent for such a curriculum to be constructed, the majority of teachers were educated in a period when knowledge and understanding of the world and our own society tended to be filtered through the 'lens' of ethnocentricism. This has meant that not only is our multicultural subject knowledge incomplete but the way we view the world is likely to be strongly influenced by language and ideas that implicitly or explicitly subjugate the knowledge base of non-European cultures. In turn, this can lead to tokenistic teaching based on stereotypical viewpoints. A second reason is the failure of QCA to provide appropriate schemes of work capable of operating as the infrastructure to encourage the development of a multicultural curriculum. A third reason is the paucity of appropriate published materials to fill the knowledge-gap. This is exacerbated by the demise of multicultural resource centres around the country caused by changes to Section 11 funding and the failure of many LEAs to recognise their value as vital sources of information. These were the very places where subjugated knowledge could be found. Underpinning these reasons is perhaps a lack of will on the part of decision makers at all levels of government to commit the resources and intellectual vigour to the construction of a curriculum that values cultural diversity and prevents racism (Macpherson 1999). From the above discussion, it would seem that a truly broad and balanced curriculum capable of reflecting the needs of a diverse society such as ours remains in the hands of individual schools and individual teachers.

Keypoints for multicultural education

Parallel to 'official' curriculum development is additional advice, provided by educators who have a long-standing commitment to multicultural education. The content of every curriculum subject needs to be grounded in a positive terrain. In part, this should include knowledge and understanding which:

- reflects the cultural, ethnic and religious diversity of Britain and the world;
- recognises that within such diversity, human beings share common values, aspirations and needs;
- provides examples of excellence from all cultures;
- demonstrates the mutual influence throughout history of countries and communities;
- realises that justice, including racial justice, within and between countries is of fundamental importance.

(Richardson and Wood 1999: 40)

Taken together, these five themes begin to sharpen our focus on what breadth and balance within the curriculum might look like. However, it must be remembered that cultural diversity does not refer only to Black and Asian communities. Other minority ethnic groups are also present in Britain and there is cultural diversity among indigenous Britons too (Brown 1998: 44). Brown rightly reminds us, with reference to Macdonald (1989), that a multiculturalism which pushes the heritage of particular groups to the margin, in favour of other groups, is likely to prove counterproductive. In view of this, a further theme is the empowerment of all individuals and groups. Raising the educational achievement of all pupils is one aspect of this theme.

Other facets include teaching that leads to an understanding of how differences of social and economic power position individuals and groups differently and that it is the uneven distribution of power, not cultural characteristics, which causes the powerful to discriminate in favour of themselves. An investigation of the uneven distribution of power could throw light on the way social structures and social discourses interact in mutually supportive ways to maintain the prevailing social hierarchy as a seemingly unalterable norm. Even though the distribution of power is uneven, we should not leave pupils with the erroneous view that the marginalised and dispossessed are completely powerless. Such a view would teach that black slaves were rescued from their plight by white philanthropists and exclude mention of the resistance and struggle against oppression of the slaves themselves.

Teaching for empowerment in a multicultural curriculum provides the scope for multiple interpretations to be achieved; teaching in an ethnocentric curriculum narrows the range of possibilities and therefore blinkers the perception of the learner. A further theme is the recognition that diversity exists within as well as between different cultures, classes, religions and genders and that individuals have multiple affiliations, which cause them to realign their individual identity over time and in different contexts. The knowledge, cognitive skills and understanding offered by such a curriculum would provide pupils with a critical awareness capable of seeing beyond superficial appearance and stereotype.

CHAPTER 3

Effective multicultural schools: raising achievement

Following a dormant period during which discussion of multicultural education, 'race' and equal opportunities 'slipped from the policy agenda' (Gillborn and Gipps 1996), a resurgence occurred in the mid to late 1990s. In some respects the re-invigorated discussion recycled issues that had been of long-term concern to multi-cultural and anti-racist educationalists. One significant difference, however, was that discussion took place at a national level and was grounded in empirical study, whereas in the 1980s, with the exception of the Swann Report, it had largely been restricted to networks of interested groups. An issue that was key to the fresh debate was the relative underachievement of particular groups of minority ethnic pupils. This was not a new phenomenon. The Rampton Committee, which had been set up in 1975, sought to investigate the reasons for the under-achievement of 'West Indian' pupils in the English school system (Rampton 1981). During the 1990s a succession of reports from government and quasi-governmental bodies suggested that other minority ethnic groups had joined African Caribbean pupils on the tail of underachievement.

A second issue of concern highlighted in these reports was racism. Although racism had been an important political issue since the 1960s, the murder of Stephen Lawrence and the tenacious struggle for justice waged by his parents, raised a mirror to the nation. The subsequent inquiry into his death brought the tragic consequences of racial violence into the living room of every home in Britain. It also exposed the sinister issue of institutional racism and forced our society to acknowledge the extent to which racial prejudice was embedded in the organisational cultures of some of our most respected institutions. To Black-British people living at the interface of ordinary existence and institutional practices, this was not a revelation. But the fact that it was 'official,' and had received such a wide hearing, meant that it would be difficult to deny the existence of institutional racism.

A third issue concerned teacher education and the view that training had failed to properly equip teachers with the necessary skills for teaching in a multicultural society. The Teacher Training Agency responded to criticism and published guidance to Higher Education Institutions (TTA 2000). Much of the guidance reflected findings of good practice contained in the reports (Blair *et al.* 1998; OFSTED 1999). Attention was given to the characteristics of successful multi-ethnic teaching and the reports emphasised the importance of ethnic monitoring of attainment, combined with strategies to raise achievement among those groups that were doing less well.

In this chapter, some of the key issues for effective teaching and learning in multicultural schools are identified by means of a review of some of the publications that emerged either from Government, or its allied quasi-government organisations, between the mid 1990s and the new millennium. The recurrent themes are summarised and major recommendations are presented in the conclusion to the chapter.

Teaching and assessing bilingual pupils

In its report entitled, *The Assessment of the Language Development of Bilingual Pupils*, OFSTED (1997), produced the findings of an HMI survey of over 50 schools and 112 LEAs, conducted a year earlier. The report identified the need for a consistent national approach to both the monitoring and assessment of attainment level of minority ethnic pupils. Under Home Office administration, data on the attainment of bilingual pupils was collected using a four-point scale which assumed a continuum of second language development, ranging from those pupils with little or no spoken English to those who spoke English fluently but required continued support in order to access the curriculum fully. HMI found that although the use of the four-point scale was widespread, LEAs applied different interpretations, making comparisons between authorities difficult. Without a national consensus, and in the absence of a moderation process, the reliability of data was flawed, which raised a question about the equitable allocation of Section 11 grant. This was not just an administrative difficulty; teachers who responded to the survey also had reservations about the scale for assessment purposes, preferring the use of diagnostic and formative methods based on National Curriculum Attainment Targets and Level Descriptions.

Teachers also preferred to use the National Curriculum as the basis for lesson and curriculum planning, making the four-point scale an administrative expedient. LEAs largely used it as a criterion for deploying Section 11 staff to schools.

Concurrent with the HMI survey, the School Curriculum and Assessment Authority (SCAA) published *Teaching English as an Additional Language: A*

Framework for Policy (SCAA 1996). Its starting point was the need for a consistent national approach to the teaching of EAL pupils. As in the OFSTED report, assessment was one of five themes identified as critical to raising the attainment of minority ethnic pupils, the other four being:

- whole school policies;
- curriculum entitlement;
- effective teaching and planning;
- effective targeting of resources at school level.

The document suggested that whole school policies needed to be based on a clear identification of pupils' needs and attainments, accompanied by effective measures to monitor progress. It advised schools to devise manageable but systematic methods of data collection, to include information about: the number and size of ethnic groups in the school; the number of pupils receiving Section 11 support (now EMTAG); the number of pupils from homes where English was not the first language and the main languages spoken by pupils. SCAA was in agreement with HMI about the most effective criterion for monitoring the progress of EAL pupils, i.e. 'The National Curriculum should . . . be the main reference point for judging the progress of the pupil as soon as possible.' (SCAA 1996: 18)

This recommendation was partially implemented in 1999 when the DfEE took control of Section 11, renaming it the Ethnic Minority and Traveller Achievement Grant (EMTAG). LEAs were asked to collect data on the comparative levels of attainment of different ethnic groups at the end of Key Stage 2 and at GCSE. The choice of these two assessment points, at 11 and at 16, perhaps reflects an historical preoccupation of the educational establishment, embedded in the 1944 Education Act, which placed summative assessment firmly in the 11+ selection tests and GCE exams. However, the required information did not provide a comprehensive picture of attainment at either local or national level, for several reasons. Firstly, it referred only to the percentages of pupils achieving Level 4 and above in English and Maths; the use of Level 4 as the benchmark obviated the need to collect comparative data about performance at Levels 1 to 3. The absence of such data obscured the degree to which some groups of pupils were underachieving. Secondly, the use of broad and sometimes erroneous 'ethnic' categories failed to identify the needs of particular ethnic groups. For example, the category 'Black-African' assumes homogeneity, whereas in reality the category subsumes diverse national and ethnic groups that may have differing needs. The same can be said of the categories 'Indian' and 'Black-Caribbean'. Thirdly, the data provided no opportunity to compare achievement on the basis of gender or social class differences. Fourthly, the fact no data was required for Key Stage 1 weakened the case for systematic ethnic monitoring of achievement in the early years of schooling.

Given these flaws, the intention to ensure 'genuine equality of opportunity for all minority ethnic groups' (DfEE 1998a) appeared unsustainable since efficient targeting of resources is unlikely in the absence of complete data. The argument for a comprehensive system of ethnic monitoring across all key stages and the 'early years' was later made by Gillborn and Mirza (2000).

SCAA recommended that the assessment of bilingual pupils should combine statutory assessments with more informal assessments of pupils over time and in a range of contexts. In order to accurately assess bilingual pupils, the importance of teachers having a knowledge of the process of EAL acquisition was recognised (Blair *et al.* 1998). The Teacher Training Agency subsequently provided guidance to Higher Education Institutions (HEIs) on this matter (TTA 2000). For practising teachers, EMTAG colleagues, some of whom have a staff development brief, are a valuable source of information.

A further recommendation made by SCAA was the systematic targeting of resources at school level to raise the attainment of minority ethnic pupils. Several suggestions about how this might be done were given, including the use of additional staff to:

• vary the size of teaching groups;
• provide additional support in the classroom;
• give focused curriculum support to pupils in withdrawal groups.

In the case of the latter, stress was put on this being for a time-limited period only. Whatever strategy is used it is important that targets are established and monitored by the class teacher and support staff; both have joint responsibility to raise levels of achievement.

The importance of home-school liaison was emphasised and in particular the expertise of bilingual staff who are able to use their linguistic knowledge to make the transition to school smoother for those pupils with little or no English and to improve the child's access to the curriculum through the first language. The language development of the bilingual child is a shared responsibility and needs to be seen as a holistic endeavour. Monolingual English speakers have a role to play in helping EAL pupils develop English by engaging them in talk. Informal conversations with adults and peers provide teachers with additional sources of information about the child's progress. The playground and the child's play offer occasions when the EAL child is less inhibited about using his or her new language, and is more likely to talk spontaneously. Reports of what the child has said, or better still, a little professional eavesdropping, can help teachers acquire a fuller picture of the child's use of English. Effective monitoring and comprehensive records allow accurate judgements to be made about the deployment of available resources. The use of human and other resources also need to take account of the demands of the curriculum at different Key Stages. The difference between English for everyday usage and its use for academic purposes is an important issue, which we return to in Chapter Five when discussing the work of Jim Cummins.

SCAA reemphasised a principle of the Education Reform Act 1988 (DES 1989: 2.2) in drawing attention to the bilingual child's curriculum entitlement. Lesson planning in multicultural classrooms needs to take account of the interconnections between subject content, learning activities and language development. Commonly used words that have a different meaning in subject specific contexts need explanation, and the syntactic and textual structures of subject specific discourses require explicit modelling. INSET material accompanying The National Literacy Strategy provides exemplars of how teachers can model writing for different purposes (DfEE 2000a *Grammar for Writing*). Language development can also be embedded in curriculum related learning through well planned collaborative group work. For the emergent bilingual child, non-verbal ways of demonstrating their thinking can enable them to show their knowledge and understanding, at a time when English is the weakest language in their linguistic repertoire. The child's first language can be an asset in the classroom, especially if an adult helper, or the teacher, speak the same language, because the curriculum can be accessed through that language, at least for part of the time. However, English, and in particular the dialect of Standard English, will ultimately be the language through which the child must demonstrate academic achievement. It must be remembered therefore that for some bilingual pupils school may be the only place where they have the opportunity to learn and use Standard English. Language policy and practice in multicultural schools must carefully balance respect for, and maintenance of, the diverse languages of their pupils and communities, while helping pupils add Standard English to their linguistic range.

Minority ethnic teachers

While SCAA concentrated on the teaching and assessment of EAL pupils, other documents addressed broader issues facing education. In a joint report, the TTA and Commission for Racial Equality (CRE) summarised the outcome of three conferences held during 1997. Concerned about the under-representation of minority ethnic groups in the teaching force, the conferences sought to identify ameliorative measures. A link was made between underachievement in school and under-representation in teacher education. By raising levels of achievement it was assumed the recruitment of minority ethnic teachers would improve. One historic reason for the under-representation of minority ethnic teachers is the institutional racism and stereotyping minority ethnic pupils experience at school which has deterred them from a career in teaching (Swann 1985: 609–10). In addition, a significant number of minority ethnic teachers were employed in Section 11 projects, where their careers were subject to continual change and the threat of redundancy (Collings 1999: 67). Hence teaching has not been viewed as a high status profession among some groups. Minority ethnic staff in multicultural schools can enhance the quality of education in several ways, including;

- affirming a positive sense of identity for minority ethnic pupils;
- improving, through discussion with colleagues, understanding of the problems faced by minority ethnic pupils;
- providing opportunities for adult–pupil talk in the child's first language;
- influencing the organisational culture and promoting equal opportunities;
- encouraging and motivating minority ethnic pupils to succeed.

(Blair *et al.* 1998: 162)

Of course, many of these functions are not exclusive to minority ethnic teachers; all teachers share a responsibility for what happens in school, just as minority ethnic teachers share with their colleagues responsibility for all pupils.

Achievement and equality

During the past decade attainment has improved across all ethnic groups (Gillborn and Mirza 2000: 26). However, the attainment of Bangladeshi, Pakistani, African Caribbean and Gypsy Traveller pupils, relative to their Indian and white counterparts, is a cause for concern (OFSTED 1999). While there are general trends, levels of achievement within these groups are uneven in some LEAs, as well as between them (Gillborn and Gipps 1996; Gillborn and Mirza 2000). In one London borough, for example, Bangladeshi pupils achieve higher SATs and GCSE results than other ethnic groups. In addition, like their white counterparts, Black and Asian girls tend to do better than boys of the same ethnic group (Mirza 1995: 182; OFSTED 1999: 7; Gillborn and Mirza 2000).

The latest information, produced by the Youth Cohort Studies, suggests that between 1997 and 2000 the number of Black and Indian students achieving 5 or more A–C grades at GCSE rose by nearly three times the national average (www. Dfee.gov.uk 2000). The Youth Cohort Studies provide the most comprehensive source of data for monitoring and cross-referencing performance over time on the basis of ethnicity, class and gender. Drawing on this longitudinal study, Gillborn and Mirza (2000) conclude that African Caribbean and Pakistani pupils have made smaller gains than other groups since 1988 and that differences of attainment are greater between different ethnic groups and social classes than between boys and girls. What these studies do not show is relative levels of attainment across key stages. Few LEAs actually collate such data but in one that does, its 1998 survey shows Black pupils attaining a level 20 per cent above the LEA average in Baseline Assessment but 21 per cent below the average at GCSE (Gillborn and Mirza 2000: 16). The importance of consistently monitoring pupils' attainment throughout their school life is emphasised in several reports. Only when accurate data is collected can trends be detected and resources targeted to raise the attainment of those who are underachieving.

Factors affecting achievement

What the various studies suggest is that reasons for differing levels of achievement between ethnic groups are complex and subject to change. Whereas the attainment of Bangladeshi and Pakistani pupils tends to improve during their school life, as stated above, there are instances when the attainment of African Caribbean pupils regresses with age. A child's social class is an influential factor in educational achievement and although since the 1980s the gap in attainment between the highest and lowest social classes has widened and is evident within ethnic groups, certain minority ethnic groups continue to underachieve even when class is taken into account (Gillborn and Mirza 2000: 64).

In an earlier study Gillborn and Gipps (1996) posited that minority ethnic pupils respond in diverse ways to school and that gender and 'race' specific stereotypes might be a cause of poorer attainment levels in some cases, particularly African Caribbean male pupils. South Asian pupils reported how some teachers viewed them in negative, patronising and stereotypical ways, particularly in relation to their language and home background. Stereotypes were especially damaging to Asian girls. Bhatti (1999: 164) found that teachers who had fixed notions of arranged marriage often stereotyped Asian girls. Girls responded either through covert forms of rebellion, by asserting their 'Asian-ness' or else experienced a lack of self-confidence. Paradoxically, young people from minority ethnic backgrounds are more likely than their white counterparts to stay at school beyond the statutory age. Gillborn and Gipps offer four possible reasons for this, including: greater motivation, parental support, to avoid unemployment and as a means of avoiding exposure to further racism in society at large.

Racial harassment

The TTA/CRE report identified racial harassment as a key issue in multicultural schools. Racial violence, especially towards Asian pupils, was found to be widespread and often went unnoticed by teachers (Gillborn and Gipps 1996). There is often a noticeable increase in racial harassment when race and immigration become political issues. The tendency is for politicians to play 'the race card', which fuels prejudice and appears to add legitimacy to those who hold prejudicial views. Prejudice and discrimination can adversely affect attainment and lead to separatism as minority groups strengthen ethnic boundaries and tighten group solidarity (Gibson 1988). Gibson also found that resistance to school occurred when minority groups perceived their culture to be undervalued and saw education as an agent of assimilation for the dominant culture. Like Macdonald, the TTA/CRE stressed that institutions and individuals, at every level in education, had a responsibility for equal opportunity policies and programmes. Explicit strategies to deal with racial harassment within whole-school policies, enabling consistent and fair treatment by all members of a school, are essential in an equal opportunity policy.

Ethnic monitoring

Although schools had a wide range of initiatives to raise attainment of all their pupils, very few of them actually had systems to effectively monitor progress and attainment. (OFSTED 1999). Without data they were unable to judge clearly the effect of their initiatives on the attainment of different minority ethnic group pupils. Primary schools in particular had scant information. This may be because of their smaller pupil numbers, making statistical comparisons difficult. Many secondary schools that collected performance data showing the relative achievements of different ethnic groups used the information as a lever to raise standards. National concern about the underachievement of specific groups, combined with a culture of target setting, ought to encourage schools to implement more proactive equal opportunity measures. However, it is critical that ethnic cohorts are accurately defined and identified and that information takes account of the interplay of the variables of class and gender, as suggested by Gillborn and Gipps (1996). OFSTED found that successful schools did monitor underachievement and senior managers held individual teachers and departments accountable for results. They reviewed and changed their curriculum and pastoral arrangements to take account of the ethnic composition of the school and its locality. Senior managers demonstrated a commitment to equal opportunities and the effective use and deployment of Section 11 and Section 488 (now EMTAG) staff, which was found to be critical to raising attainment.

OFSTED identified a third of LEAs, mostly in London and metropolitan areas, with comprehensive systems to monitor minority ethnic attainment. Gillborn and Gipps (1996: 79) make the point that ethnic diversity is not a 'cities only issue' and that standards are unlikely to rise consistently across the country unless all LEAs collect accurate data and act upon the findings.

Social behaviour

Good race relations in school are characterised by an open ethos in which pupils share concerns and are involved, devising problem solving strategies. Staff are vigilant and address rising tension quickly. Those schools where minority ethnic pupils flourished recognised and understood the social hostility that those pupils faced and implemented strategies to raise confidence and self-esteem by countering stereotypes (OFSTED 1999).

Characteristics of successful multi-ethnic schools

In a comprehensive report Blair *et al.* (1998) also identified characteristics of successful multi-ethnic schools. Their sample included schools where at least 10 per cent of pupils came from the most disadvantaged minority ethnic groups. The chosen schools either achieved GCSE results above the national average, showed steady improvement or performed better than similar schools. Two factors stood out as essential to their success. Firstly, they were 'listening' schools; that is, staff took time to understand the perspectives of pupils and their parents and used feedback to re-appraise institutional practices and develop an inclusive curriculum. The schools acknowledged the dynamic and culturally diverse nature of their local communities. They recognised the importance of being what Harold Rosen termed 'ethnographic centres' (1988) ones in which people were: 'learning together as a micro-society about values: equity, fairness, respect, the management of conflicting interests, adaptability, and ways of applying these to daily practice.' (Blair *et al.* 1998: 50).

Within these micro-societies, identities are created and recreated, relationships transformed and cultural meanings are redefined as lives change with the interplay of ethnicity, gender, and class. Secondly, successful schools had sufficient resources and flexibility to deploy staff to meet the changing needs of learners.

In addition to these two central points, other features of successful schools were identified, including:

- strong leadership on equality issues;
- good community links;
- working with the 'whole child';
- clarity of purpose in dealing with racist bullying;
- strategies to avoid exclusions;
- high expectations of teachers and pupils;
- clear systems of monitoring progress and targeting resources;
- ethnic monitoring to ensure equality of opportunity.

In contrast unsuccessful multi-ethnic schools were ones where low expectations led to underachievement; where racism and stereotyping prevailed and where there was lack of respect for pupils and parents, accompanied by poor communication with home. Blair *et al.* saw the importance of spreading good practice, and in the spirit of their report it is worth putting flesh on their findings here.

Leadership

Successful multi-ethnic schools were characterised by leaders who possessed a clear view of equal opportunities and who were able to convince their staff of the clarity of their vision. They tended to be leaders who listened to staff, parents and pupils and who understood the socio-political factors that influenced the lives of their pupils and the community.

Relationships

As well as listening to the views of parents and pupils, effective schools used feedback to review and adapt school practices. They were proactive in developing links in the community and making school welcoming and accessible for all parents. Attempts were made to understand individual pupils and to provide the necessary academic and pastoral support to enable pupils to succeed. Allegations of racism were followed up by means of clearly understood, whole-school procedures and explicit behaviour policies were designed to minimise the need for exclusions.

Expectations

Successful schools had high expectations of staff and pupils. All pupils, irrespective of learning needs, were treated as potential high achievers and were supported accordingly. Homework clubs were available to pupils. Poorly motivated pupils were encouraged through well-structured mentoring schemes with precise aims and objectives.

Monitoring

Monitoring achievement by gender and ethnicity enabled any disparities between boys and girls within the same ethnic group as well as across subject boundaries to be identified. Where under-achievement was apparent, strategies were implemented to reverse trends. Ethnic monitoring enabled schools to deal with precise details instead of reacting to needs based on stereotypical assumptions.

Curriculum

The curriculum is central to education; it provides numerous opportunities for showing respect for the cultural and personal identities of pupils (Richardson and Wood 1999: 40). Effective schools demonstrate this by including within the curriculum the histories, languages, religions and cultures of their pupils. Given that the curriculum is an indicator of the way a society views itself (Gaine and George, 1999: 68); a multicultural curriculum is applicable to all schools.

The needs of specific groups

Successful schools forge close relationships between mainstream teachers and support staff. Through liaison, colleagues share understanding of the specific needs of particular minority ethnic groups. The linguistic expertise of bilingual colleagues is used to assess bilingual pupils in order to differentiate EAL needs from special educational needs, and thereby target specialist resources appropriately. The experience of the African-Caribbean community in the education system was taken into account when addressing provision for Black pupils and intensive induction courses were provided for pupils new to English.

Summary

The various reports provide substantial evidence of successful teaching in multicultural schools and classrooms. They have helped to clarify the issues that need to be addressed and have reflected the nature of an inclusive education for social justice. The central themes of such an education take account of, and provide for, the development of individual and collective identities freed from the dehumanising mask of stereotype. This requires schools to listen to pupils and parents alike and to understand the social processes that are at work in the construction of identity. They also need to discern how pupils respond differently to those social processes and how individuals and groups resist coercive pressure, negative attitudes and actions. In order to become good 'listening institutions' schools need effective two-way communication with parents and local communities.

Low expectations tether individuals and groups to the 'tail of under-achievement' but successful schools aim to focus attention not only on the potential of every child to succeed but on processes to effectively 'scaffold' higher levels of achievement for all. Part of that scaffolding requires institutions to monitor differential patterns of achievement between groups; to set targets; to target resources appropriately and to be innovative with teaching and learning strategies. Successful schools are led by head teachers and senior managers who understand equal opportunity issues and incorporate that understanding in their educational vision and practice. The curriculum is inclusive of diverse cultural, linguistic, religious and ethnic identities and demonstrates, through its knowledge base the contribution made to civilisation and human achievement by individuals and societies across the world.

CHAPTER 4

Schools in action: two case studies

The curriculum may be the backbone of teaching and learning in school but no matter how important we consider it there are other factors that contribute to a child's education. In Chapter Two one of the De Montfort students referred to her school's open ethos, which enabled pupils to share their cultural experience. The collective values, attitudes and vision of teachers inform expectations of how people should relate to one another in classrooms and in school generally. School is one place where young people develop a sense of their own worth in relation to others. A school's ethos, along with its practices and procedures, is a key element in this development of individual and social identity. In recent years schools have been given greater autonomy to manage their own affairs and while they may be highly organised institutions, they are not logistical islands. Effective schools recognise the permeability of boundaries. A school has a symbiotic relationship to its community. Good schools, therefore, recognise that children's learning takes place outside as well as inside the school grounds and put in place procedures to tap this learning, or to enhance it. Parents, family and community are as central to children's development and achievement as teachers are. Education is a social phenomenon and a network of social factors that interact with the individual's personal attributes influence the development of each child.

This discussion reflects that which appeared in Chapter Three when reviewing recent evidence of the education of minority ethnic pupils in Britain. In short, educational achievement is dependent upon a complex array of interacting factors. Recent case studies of schools across Europe support the view that a multi-level approach, which integrates all the key players and influences on a child's education, provides the most effective means of scaffolding children's learning, leading to raised levels of achievement (Green 1999). The use of case study as a way of exemplifying good practice is becoming more common in the literature (Blair *et al.*

1998; DfEE 2000b). In this chapter the use of case study in research is briefly analysed. This analysis is followed by case studies of two schools; Leatfield Lower School and Rosehedge Infants School.

The case for case studies

The term 'case study' is a generic one and covers various research methods that are used to investigate often complex interacting variables within a given context (Hitchcock and Hughes 1995: 316). Case study involves a bounded focus, defined in time and space, in which particular events are scrutinised in a 'systematic critical search for truths' (Bassey 1995: 110–111). The unique value of case studies is their potential to reveal important ideas through the study of real lives and real events in a way that statistical data cannot (Cohen *et al.* 2000: 181). Typical methods of research include; documentation, file data, interviews, site visits, direct observation, participant observation and physical artefacts (Anderson and Arsenault 1998: 155). Clearly, these methods place a heavy emphasis on the interpretative skills of the researcher. In addition, 'the case' immerses the researcher in the 'new culture' (Delamont 1992: 8); she or he becomes part of it, and must, therefore, retain a sense of her or his own influence on the findings. By means of critical self reflection, the researcher must recognise, understand and acknowledge the ways in which their position within the research interacts with the phenomenon that is being studied (Hammersley and Atkinson 1983, cited in Delamont 1992). Using appropriate methods the researcher collects data from a range of sources including the subjective accounts (Hammersley 1989: 93). It is essential, therefore, that 'key players', 'key situations' and 'critical incidents in the life of the case' (Hitchcock and Hughes 1995: 319) are identified early so that the researcher may locate, describe, analyse and ultimately present findings around the essential themes and variables evident in the case. Hitchcock and Hughes identify key characteristics that case studies are likely to have, including:

- a concern with the rich and vivid description of event within the case;
- a chronological narrative of events within the case;
- an internal debate between the description of events and the analysis of events;
- a focus upon particular individual actors or groups of actors and their perceptions;
- a focus upon particular events within the case;
- the integral involvement of the researcher in the case;
- a way of presenting the case which is able to capture the richness of the situation.

(Hitchcock and Hughes 1995: 317)

Given the attention to detail and the emphasis on describing the way things happen in particular instances, case studies are a useful vehicle for sharing practice between practitioners in different settings. This is especially so when the focus of attention is on alternative ways of doing things within institutions that share similar cultural characteristics (Hitchcock and Hughes 1995: 322). The publication of case studies of multi-ethnic schools which are striving to improve and make more relevant the education they provide, contributes to the quest for higher educational standards. Schools located in diverse multicultural areas that are experiencing almost continual social and economic change need to understand such change and the effect on people's lives, as well as upon the institutions in which those social lives are played out. Social behaviour and cultural practices do not remain static, nor are they uniform within particular ethnic groups. Therefore, there is continual need to study, analyse and present data that seeks to inform teachers of possible ways to respond to new social and cultural realities. Case studies of successful practice provide one means of spreading the word.

The two cases in question

The two schools presented were chosen because they have good reputations among professionals in their locality for their approach to multicultural education and raising attainment. I began by interviewing each head teacher to explore the characteristics of her school and the practices she deemed to be particularly relevant to raising achievement and/or developing a multicultural or inclusive approach. During these interviews critical events in the history of each school were identified, along with 'key players'. In addition to transcribed material, field notes of observations and specific artefacts and documentary information were the main ways in which data were collected. Each school was visited several times. Soon after each visit data were sifted and written up as a draft of the final presentation. The drafts were shown to the respective head teachers, who checked them for factual accuracy and verified my interpretation of meanings. This proved to be a particularly useful strategy for two reasons. Firstly, the drafts triggered fresh data or modified existing data as information missed in the initial interview was added. They also raised questions on issues and events that required further clarification. Secondly, 'key players' in each school, notably the head teacher, were fully involved, not only in providing information, but also in its analysis. By means of this collaborative approach, they were able to retain partial ownership of the way information about their school was presented to a wider audience. Not only was there an almost seamless development of the research and the presentation of its findings, but also ethical issues around the relative positions of the researcher and respondent were integral to the research process.

Leatfield case study

Background

Leatfield Lower School is bounded by an industrial area, a railway embankment and a residential area of small back-to-back Victorian houses. In common with many similar urban schools, its pupils come from relatively poor socio-economic backgrounds. 75 per cent of pupils speak English as an Additional Language. Two minority ethnic groups are represented within the school. The larger of the groups is Sikh, Panjabi speakers and the other is Muslim, Sylheti speakers. The remaining 25 per cent of pupils include one Turkish child and two children from the former Yugloslavia amongst monolingual English children.

Leatfield was established in 1996 when two former schools were amalgamated. Both schools had falling rolls and the local authority took the decision to open a new school under a new head teacher. In addition to the organisational difficulties that usually accompany school amalgamation, there was an additional dimension to be considered. The schools had served two different minority ethnic communities and careful management was needed to integrate the largely Bangladeshi contingent of one school with the predominantly Sikh community of the other. Both schools had received additional support from the Area Minority Support Service (MASS).

The new head teacher had two imperatives for her new cohort of pupils. One was to raise the self-esteem of individual pupils within a positive school climate and the other was to raise levels of academic achievement. Shortly after the amalgamation significant changes took place in the management of MASS, which impinged on the school's Development Plan. As the management of MASS changed and new organisational structures were introduced, the amount of support given to the school also changed. In effect, support has been cut from two teachers and one full-time equivalent learning support assistant to the current level of 0.8 and 0.5 respectively. In addition, the quality of support from MASS was questionable. The 1998 inspection report on the school commented: 'While there is evidence that pupils with English as an additional language make progress in gaining access to the curriculum, more progress could be made if their needs were targeted more specifically.'

One of the school's Key Issues, therefore, focused on using Section 11 staff more effectively in order to raise the attainment of EAL pupils, which prompted the school to re-evaluate the way MASS colleagues were deployed. As a result, instead of the MASS teacher supporting pupils across the school, it was decided to concentrate support on a specific group of EAL pupils. How this group was selected, the nature of support given to the group and the outcome in terms of pupils' achievements is described below.

Despite internal changes and an uncertain external environment, several years after the merger Leatfield is a thriving, purposeful educational community where improving levels of academic achievement are evident. The 1999 Key Stage 2 results in mathematics show a 27 per cent improvement over those of 1997. This was accompanied by improvements in reading comprehension and writing of 4 per cent and 12 per cent respectively. This case study describes and analyses several features of the school that appear to have contributed to this achievement.

First impressions

The first time visitor to Leatfield cannot avoid the obvious multicultural composition of the school. Amidst notices in English are ones written in Gurmurkhi, the Panjabi script used by Sikhs. The wider community is acknowledged by means of a poster advertising a forthcoming cultural event involving a classical Indian dancer, who is also the parent of a child at the school. On one noticeboard are colour photographs of the staff: English, Asian and African Caribbean colleagues are represented among both teaching and non-teaching staff. Equally evident is the level of deprivation experienced by some of Leatfield's pupils. While waiting in the foyer for my first meeting with the head teacher, I could see the school secretary tending a little girl who had been brought in late by her mother. The girl wore a pair of trainers with broken laces, which the secretary did her best to repair. As she chatted to the girl she asked if she had eaten breakfast that morning. The girl silently replied by shaking her head.

Class organisation and curriculum delivery

There are seven classes at Leatfield, covering two Key Stages. The school operates a mixed ability, vertically grouped class structure with three classes in each Key Stage and a separate Reception Class. In part, the decision to have mixed age classes was an organisational expedient, there being an insufficient number of pupils in any one year group to create several complete classes. But it was also done to create small teams of teachers in each Key Stage who were able to collaborate and share subject expertise during the planning and evaluation stages of curriculum delivery, teaching and learning. The member of the Key Stage team who has the greatest knowledge in that subject plans each subject. In this way the planning stage is made less bureaucratic and the team is able to deliver a consistent curriculum, both in terms of content and approach. Although the general organisation of classes is mixed ability, pupils are put into sets for literacy and numeracy, and in Key Stage 1 approximately 14 EAL pupils form a fourth group that is taught by the MASS teacher. As in most schools following the introduction of the Literacy and

Numeracy Strategies the morning sessions are devoted to these aspects of the curriculum with afternoon sessions given over to Science and the Foundation subjects. During the afternoon sessions the MASS teacher works alongside class teachers in an open plan setting giving general support but still retaining a specific focus on the 14 pupils from the morning session.

Rather than timetabling separate Foundation subjects, teaching is delivered in blocked units so that each week there is a specific subject focus. This enables teachers and pupils to explore an aspect of the curriculum in depth and enables pupils to experience the benefits of in depth learning. It also means that sufficient time can be given to extended writing, which is not possible within the prescribed structure of the Literacy Strategy. Although this approach to the curriculum may narrow the range of what is taught within each subject, it does enable teachers to ensure continuity and progression in learning within a specific time frame. Even though several weeks elapse between blocked units of work in a subject, close monitoring suggests that because pupils have learned the subject in depth they are able to recall knowledge and transfer concepts and skills across the time lapse.

The EAL target group

Charged with the task of raising the attainment of EAL pupils, the Key Stage 1 team identify those pupils who are on, or just below, the borderline of Level 1 and Level 2c in English and Maths. These pupils then form the group to be taught literacy and numeracy by the MASS teacher. Initially, the teacher, who had worked at the school for ten years and had witnessed many changes, was sceptical about the efficacy of such a strategy, believing that EAL pupils should always be taught in the mainstream classroom, where they would hear good models of English. However, she reported that after a term her view changed because she saw the benefits of the approach. She noted that the children in the group appeared more confident and she attributed this change to three factors.

Firstly, she speculated that in the mainstream class these children lacked confidence because they perceived other children to be brighter than they were and therefore became reluctant to speak. In the smaller group they had more one-to-one contact and more opportunity to talk. Secondly, she adapted the planning to meet the needs of the pupils. Although, the class was vertically grouped, she followed the Year 1 scheme for literacy and numeracy, which enabled the Year 2 pupils to consolidate their learning. Thirdly, she used a wide linguistic repertoire for teaching, including her own first language, Panjabi, but also Hindi, Gujerati and English. Many of the Bangladeshi pupils knew Hindi, in addition to their own language, Sylheti, which the teacher did not speak. The MASS teacher explained the reason why she thought it important to make the teaching multilingual:

... if you don't use their language ... they won't be very comfortable ... they won't understand ... if they don't understand they won't be interested. I read them stories and tell them the meanings in Panjabi, and Hindi, or Gujerati and they say, 'Oh, it's so easy!'. When they understand, they are interested and then they are involved.

(taped interview)

It is clear from this illustration that for bilingual children the use of a home language as the medium for teaching and learning can be not only a key that unlocks their motivation but a way of enabling them to develop concepts through a language other than English, at a time in their school lives when they feel more comfortable in that language. In this way they have greater access to the curriculum than they might otherwise have had in the mainstream classroom, where the EMTAG teacher's help would have been more 'thinly spread', not just within one class but across several, as had been the practice at the time of the OFSTED inspection.

Self-esteem

Raising children's self-esteem was seen by the head teacher as an imperative prerequisite to effective learning:

... self-esteem must come first. If you don't have children who feel comfortable and confident and are prepared to take risks then you haven't got a hope of raising achievement ... For us in school trying to get the right atmosphere is important ...

(taped interview)

It was a belief that could be detected in the general ethos and practices of the school. On one noticeboard there was a display entitled 'Special Person'. Seven colour photographs of randomly selected pupils were proudly displayed under an explanation that read:

Every week one person from each class is chosen to be the SPECIAL PERSON of the week. The special person will have their picture taken for the lobby display; they will receive a special badge and a certificate of compliments from their class. Throughout the week, the special people will be given other privileges to help make this week one to remember. Everyone, staff and children, will have a turn at being special at some time during the year.

While each child had their photograph taken by the head teacher, the rest of the class had circle time. This time was used to elicit from the child's classmates their positive perceptions of him or her, which were recorded and given to the child on a special certificate. At other times pupils were also encouraged to evaluate aspects of their experience at school. On one such occasion, the responses from pupils suggested dissatisfaction about the amount of feedback they were receiving from teachers, which prompted staff to review the school's marking policy.

Curriculum, teaching and learning

The school views its multicultural intake as a positive resource for learning both within the context of the classroom and in terms of the wider society. With three distinct ethnic groups on roll, the emphasis is on sharing experiences so that diversity is acknowledged without any group being left marginalised:

> We have always taken the view that we have a wealth of information within our community that we can all learn and benefit from so we try to adapt the curriculum to take count of what is an extra resource . . .
>
> (head teacher: taped interview)

One advantage for the school of its location in a multiculural community was the availability of different places of worship. Churches, a gurudwara and a mosque were all within easy access of the school. However, it was acknowledged that some of the more prescriptive aspects of the curriculum such as the National Literacy Strategy allowed little room for manoeuvre. Nevertheless, the school had developed its literacy base to include a wide range of multicultural books and its library had been 'audited' by the staff from the local school library service. As a result, books depicting stereotypical images had been discarded.

Alongside the multicultural dimension of the curriculum there was renewed emphasis on learning and pedagogy, which the school had identified in its development plan. The head teacher explained:

> . . . we have got to the point now where we are comfortable with the content [of the curriculum] and we are comfortable with creating an ethos that encourages children to do their best . . . we have spent so many years worrying about content that we have actually lost what's happening about how children learn and how teachers teach . . . now we are moving back again . . . a curriculum based around how children learn is important.
>
> (head teacher: taped interview)

Home–school links

Home–school liaison is an important issue for the school. Before the new school opened, the headteacher offered each family a meeting, either in school or at their home. Before entry to school, each child and his or her family is visited at home by the MASS teacher and the nursery nurse. The visits provide an opportunity to initiate what the school hopes to be an effective partnership between teachers and parents. Asha explained that these initial visits often proved to be very informative. Parents openly talked about their child's capabilities and any concerns they had. School staff reciprocated by informing parents about school and what their child would be doing. These visits often had a lasting effect on pupils: '. . . children see it as important too sometimes. In Year 4 they remember the first time we visited their home . . . they feel comfortable before they come to school.' (MASS teacher, taped interview).

Pre-entry visits are not the only home visits that are made by the school. Informal home visits also take place when important issues occur and it is recognised that the family may be unable or reluctant to come into school. Inability or failure to attend parent–teacher consultations might also be followed by a home visit. By being proactive the school managed to communicate with the vast majority of its parents. It was an approach that was found to be more efficient and effective than translating letters to be sent home, which could take a significant amount of time from teaching. It was also found that those parents who could not read English tended to be illiterate in their first language.

Rosehedge Infants School

Background

Rosehedge Infants shares its site with two other schools: a Special School and a Nursery, with which it has close links. Set in a 'leafy' environment, one might be deceived into thinking the school's catchment covered a middle class area. In winter, when the trees are bare, the scrap yard, which borders one side of the playground, is a symbolic reminder that this is not an affluent community. Although relatively few pupils have free school meals, which is the Government's usual indicator of poverty, the low take-up is largely for cultural and religious reasons rather than socio-economic one.

The proportion of minority ethnic pupils on its school roll of 160 fluctuates between 50 and 60 per cent. The school is located in a 'mobile' community and in any one year there is a turnover of approximately 25 per cent of pupils. The head teacher identified five causes of what she called 'turbulence'. Firstly, within the catchment area is a women's refuge with a constantly changing clientele. Secondly, the area includes a number of hotels, which accommodate refugee families. These are invariably short stays pending the local authority's allocation of suitable permanent housing, usually outside the school's catchment area. Thirdly, the school serves a council estate where tenancies, for some families, tend to be short-term. Situated behind the school is a residential area of mainly Victorian and Edwardian two and three bedroom houses, occupied by young families. As these families expand they tend to move from the area in favour of larger houses elsewhere. The fifth reason for the annual turnover of pupils is extended holidays, which can be for as long as a year in duration. Some Gujerati families (the school's largest minority ethnic group) tend to take extended holidays visiting family abroad, which last several months, while some Bangladeshi families tend to spend even longer periods away.

In addition to Gujerati and Bangladeshi heritage children, the school attracts Hindu Panjabi pupils, African Caribbean pupils, mostly from Jamaica, French speaking children from Africa, as well as Ibo speakers and Albanian refugee children.

At the time of the current head teacher's appointment, four years ago, the school was well established within the community. However, its SATs results were depressed, a state of affairs that has since been reversed. The school now achieves end of Key Stage 1 results that are roughly in line with the national average.

Most of the school's staff is White-British but the team of nine teachers includes one African Caribbean teacher. In addition, two Asian language assistants are employed through EMTAG funding. Despite the will to make the staff more representative of the school's population, by advertising locally and nationally in the minority ethnic press and social centres frequented by minority ethnic groups, attempts have been frustrated by a dearth of suitably qualified candidates. This lack of minority ethnic teachers reflects the concern expressed by the TTA and the CRE about the low recruitment levels of minority ethnic students to Schools of Education in universities; a point referred to in Chapter Two. In the head teacher's view the problem is caused by the generally low status of teaching. However, the school is committed to broadening its staff profile and has retained this as a target in its development plan.

First impressions

Schools convey messages about the kind of institutions they are by what they choose to show about themselves, and the ways in which they show it. Rosehedge Infants is housed in an unassuming building and in a similar fashion the school is very matter of fact about its identity. Above the entrance are two simple signs, one in English and the other in Gujerati. Both signs read 'Main Entrance'. On the door is an engraved metal plate which says 'Welcome' in 22 languages. Apart from the obvious ethnic diversity of the pupils who play happily together in the play area, which is equipped with wooden play equipment, there are simple indications that this is a multicultural school committed to a pluralistic philosophy. A refrain used by the headteacher during our interview was 'difference is good' and reminders of this commitment are evident in the staffroom where copies of the SHAP Calendar

(SHAP 1999) and the CRE's Code of Practice for the Elimination of Racial Discrimination in Education (CRE 1989) hang alongside more general booklets on the staff noticebaord.

Deployment of EMTAG staff

Compared to Leatfield School, Rosehedge Infants has a more generous allocation of EMTAG staff. In addition to one full-time teacher and a 0.4 full-time equivalent (fte), it also has one full-time English-Gujerati classroom assistant and 0.4 fte English-Bengali classroom assistant. In April 2000 the school lost its funding for a 0.2 fte English-Panjabi assistant. The school is also able to call on additional funding from the LEA, amounting to 20 hours of staff time. This resource enables refugee children to be supported at a time when they can be emotionally vulnerable and in need of intensive help to orientate themselves in a new environment.

The head teacher favoured the devolution of EMTAG money to the school. Although it meant an increase in administration, it enables her to tailor support to the needs of the school and general learning patterns of pupils. In the case of part-time staff it means that time can be allocated in the morning sessions when children are more alert.

The 0.4 fte teacher is an early years specialist who works with Reception age children. Some cohorts of children include many that have not had Nursery experience and therefore a particular emphasis of her work is home–school liaison. The percentage of minority ethnic pupils who have been to the Nursery can fluctuate from year to year and often depends on parents' knowledge, or lack of it, of pre-statutory age provision. The Nursery draws children from surrounding villages as well as the immediate locality. Village parents tend to be more knowledgeable of the education system and apply for places early. When minority ethnic parents do not have the same cultural capital as their white middle class counterparts, children from minority ethnic backgrounds may be disadvantaged in the early years of schooling. In the interests of equal opportunities, there is clearly a need for more proactive work on the part of local authorities to inform all parents of their entitlement to state provision for the under-fives.

The teacher also helps provide a rich curriculum and assists emergent bilingual pupils to develop early skills in English. The two language assistants, who are allocated to classes on the basis of children's language needs, support this. Normally, time is fairly evenly distributed across the various classes. The full-time EMTAG teacher, who has worked at the school for 20 years, focuses on Years 1 and 2. Her main brief is to help raise achievement, but she also undertakes some home visits, prepares individualised packs of work for children leaving on extended holidays and manages the other EMTAG staff.

Class teachers and EMTAG staff operate a flexible, professional working relationship. Essentially, at the planning stage, they ask the question, 'What do we want pupils to learn?' and then 'How can we best use our EMTAG resources to achieve this?' Depending on learning objectives and the particular needs of pupils, class teachers and EMTAG colleagues then identify viable strategies and define their respective roles. Hence, learning is placed at the heart of the logistics of resources.

EMTAG staff then, adopt a variety of approaches to in-class support. One approach involves the EMTAG teacher and class teacher taking half the class each. On other occasions as one teacher takes the lead the other focuses on a specific group of pupils. The EMTAG teacher also has a training role and sometimes models lessons with the whole class, particularly when the school recruits a new class teacher. Although the emphasis is on in-class support, occasionally pupils are withdrawn for intensive one to one support.

Home, school and community

The school has a long history of involvement in the local community. One teacher is an active member of the local African Caribbean Association and the school's full-time EMTAG teacher has developed close links with the Gujerati community. The head teacher makes positive attempts to recruit from the locality, believing it to be one way of developing good communication between school and community. The majority of staff at the school live locally and the governing body is representative of the ethnic diversity of the school. Teachers at the school often attend functions at the mandeer (Hindu Temple) as well as other events in the community. The major festivals of the religions represented, both in the school and the community at large, are celebrated annually and attract parents from all faiths, even when the festival is not one celebrated in their own religion. Indeed, celebration is one way in which the school seems to maintain a sense of its collective self. In the entrance to the school is a colourful picture of balloons rising into the air surrounded by jubilant children and adults. The title to the picture is ' Celebrating our OFSTED Inspection Report – March 1998'. Attached to each balloon is a pink ticket with the name of a child and a quote from the inspector's report.

The style and content of the monthly newsletter to parents similarly conveys the spirit of the school as a collective enterprise. As well as thanking parents and friends of the school for their help with a range of fund raising initiatives, it referred to attendance at a SATs evening in a very upbeat way. It invited parents to offer suggestions about future improvements to the playground and reflected on parents' positive feedback about last term's curriculum letter. A new curriculum letter was attached to the general newsletter. It informed parents about curriculum topics to be covered by each year group over the coming half term, and offered advice on how they could best help their children at home. An example of the advice given included the following for parents of Reception pupils: 'At home you can support your child by continuing to help them learn their weekly words. You can also visit the local shops and supermarket and perhaps help your child make a shopping list before you go.'

In a simple but subtle way such tips give guidance to those parents whose recollections of early years schooling may be hazy or who, in the case of some minority ethnic parents, have been educated in school systems where there is no tradition of home–school links. Schools that want to further the inclusion of parents in their children's development by demonstrating how normal domestic routines can be educational might find the video *Home – The Starting Point* useful (Focus in Education Productions 1994). The video could be a useful addition at meetings for 'new parents'.

Curriculum

Given the school's ethos, it is not surprising that the head teacher is fully supportive of a broad curriculum. In her view, to be educated means to have a broad vision. It therefore follows that a broad curriculum must be inclusive of knowledge and concepts derived from the breadth of human experience. Without labelling it as such, the school's view is that a broad curriculum must, by its very nature, be a multicultural one. The school makes diversity integral to the curriculum because:

> If they (multicultural elements) are a 'bolt on' when the curriculum is under pressure they fall off whereas, if they are an integral part, when the curriculum is under pressure they remain as rock solid bits. Celebrations of religious festivals are, therefore, part of the curriculum, as is Black History Week.
>
> (head teacher, taped interview)

The head teacher made the point that schools committed to a curriculum that is inclusive of contributions to our national and world community must look beyond the confines of the National Curriculum and schemes of work produced by QCA.

Monitoring achievement

The school tracks and sets targets for individual pupils. Monitoring by ethnic group has proven difficult because the pupil population is so diverse, making statistical comparisons impracticable. There have been no discernible patterns in achievement between different groups of pupils over the past four years. For example, last year all pupils achieving Level 3 in SATs were girls but this year they were all boys. While the school is mindful of monitoring to ensure no group is discriminated against, it is equally aware that multiple variables impinge on variations in achievement. Variables of gender, ethnicity and class not only cut across one another but are made more complex by the movement of families in and out of the community, as well as social and domestic problems specific to individual families. The 'turbulence factor' has a profound effect on the school's published results. Of 60 pupils who started in the Reception class 32 had left the school to be replaced by others by the time of the SATs. The remaining 28 pupils, who had received nine full terms of education at the school did significantly better in the SATs than the newcomers. Approximately 90 per cent of the original cohort achieved Level 2 or above. This is a significant achievement but one that is likely to be masked by the school's position in the league tables.

Self-esteem

The school's Mission Statement reads: 'At Rosehedge Infants School we will maintain confidence in, and commitment to, our school aims; striving together to raise the expectations of, and provision for, our diverse school community.'

The statement reflects an inclusive philosophy that runs to the very heart of the school. It is a community that is both diverse and unified; one where difference is acceptable and accepted. The head teacher related an anecdote that epitomises the effect of the school's ethos on the way children relate to one another.

One child, the son of a mum from Peru and an English father, liked the multi-coloured patchwork pantaloons his mum had made for herself and asked if she would make a similar pair for him, which she did. His father was aghast when the son wanted to wear the brightly coloured trousers to school. 'The children will laugh at him wearing those,' he claimed. 'No they won't,' replied the mother. 'It's not that kind of school.' The boy wore the trousers to school. No one laughed.

As is evident from this story the school does not have a uniform, which does not go down well with a tiny minority of local parents who send their children to other schools for this very reason. However, the view taken in the school is that: 'uniform is a potent symbol of conformity' and its absence is, 'one of the most powerful ways of avoiding bullying'. (Head teacher, taped interview).

The story of the boy and his colourful trousers is emblematic of this view. In addition to designated curriculum time for PSHE, the school community lives its philosophy of 'difference is good'. It appears to be a philosophy that is widely supported by the parents who send their children to the school.

End note

Many of the positive characteristics of these two schools are generic to effective schools everywhere: good home school relations; the promotion of self-esteem; and attempts to create meaningful contexts for learning by reflecting and building upon children's experiences. But the success of these multi-ethnic schools is largely due to proactive strategies to achieve positive educational outcomes, accompanied by the energy and resourcefulness of the respective head teachers and staff. In a relatively short space of time both schools have raised the educational achievement of minority ethnic pupils. This appears to have been achieved by integrating several factors. These include: the systematic monitoring of pupils; precise targeting of additional support; utilising the expertise of bilingual colleagues; proactive communication with parents and carers; and the valuing of individuality within the parameters of culture.

The case studies also raise several issues that need to be addressed at national level. The first of these concerns the publication of results as league tables. Successive governments have placed great emphasis on the publication of end of key stage results and GCSEs as part of the process of public accountability. However, despite attempts to find ways of representing a school's value-added contribution to achievement, results continue to be presented as crude data. In addition, the figures mask the social conditions under which particular schools operate. The effect on a school's results of a highly mobile community with attendant social problems is not transparent in the published figures. League tables therefore do not present schools' achievements to the public in an equitable way. In view of the fact that parents may make judgements of schools' performances on the basis of results, which may be flawed by omission and lack of information, multi-ethnic schools in areas of transient population may lose the support of the more stable element of the community. Once a school falls into the downward spiral of reduced pupil numbers with a concomitant loss of funding, cuts in staff have to be made in order to balance the budget. The knock-on effects often involve reorganisation and lower staff morale, which can ultimately affect the atmosphere within the school and pupils' learning. Neither of the case study schools were in this situation but other multi-ethnic schools might not be so fortunate.

There was also a lack of equity in the way Rosehedge Infants was compared to other schools in its PANDA group. Schools are clustered in PANDAs on the basis of shared characteristics, the number of children receiving free school meals being one attribute. At Rosehedge Infants some children who were eligible to receive free school meals did not apply for them for dietary reasons linked to religious or cultural factors. As a result, the school was grouped with ones in more affluent areas and had its performance compared with theirs. Had the content and preparation of meals been appropriate to the school's multi-ethnic pupils, the take-up rate of free school meals might have been greater, which could have put the school in a different PANDA group; one that would have enabled a more equitable comparison to be made.

Even when multi-ethnic schools in less affluent areas are effective in raising achievement, the significance of their educational outcomes may be masked by the way they are forced to make themselves accountable to the public. What are, in essence, good schools may appear mediocre or poor, in the public domain. It may be the case, therefore, that colleagues in multi-ethnic schools work harder to generate a positive view of their pupils' achievements than colleagues in schools in affluent areas. In this way, a flawed system of public accountability could mean that discrimination becomes institutionalised.

CHAPTER 5

The multilingual classroom: language and power

For some children school can be a frightening place. Several years ago a former colleague of mine, Sue Crabbe, recorded some British-Bangladeshi children talking during a project she had initiated on names and name-calling. Eventually, the conversation turned to a name that had a very clear and painful meaning for them. Some readers may have heard the word used in common parlance, thinking it to be an innocuous noun.

Aysha   They call me 'paki' in class too. They were throwing books and puzzles. I got on the floor to pick up the puzzle and put it back in the bag. One of them kicked me. My teacher said she couldn't help as they were being naughty to her. Then one of them tore my work and tried to cut my hair with scissors. I want to go outside the classroom to work. I don't want to come to school.

Rafiq   It makes me feel horrible inside when they call me 'paki' . . .

Aysha   When they call me 'paki' I feel angry. I feel like hitting and kicking them. I say nothing . . .

Iqubal   I just try to take no notice. My mum says ignore them. Don't listen, that way I can cope.

Rafiq   They knock on our door and run away. They throw mud and stones at my house.

Farzana They broke our upstairs window. They shout 'fucking paki' at my little brother when he goes out in the street. That's why he doesn't play out.

Aysha   I took my Aunty's baby to the park when she came. I put her in the baby swing. Then a boy came and threw a stone at the baby. I had to take my baby out quickly and very quickly run home with her and shut my door hard.

Language is never neutral. Words are imbued with meaning. They are filled with value because they derive their full semantic content and texture from the social contexts in which they are used. Attitudes, emotions and actions fix relationships between speakers and help to define their language. Semantic content is informed by the relative positions of the speakers and in turn the words used influence their future position, which includes the status quo. Racist language is cyclical. It always places one speaker in a superior position; a position informed by an assumption of superiority. For the other 'speaker' silence may be the only way to cope, or else, flight to security. In 'shutting the door hard' Aysha has given us a metaphor that expresses the powerful effect of racist language. At six years old she, and her peer group, understood the full meaning of 'paki'. It comes with stones thrown at babies, a kick aimed at a child on the floor, a dangerous walk in the street and ends with wanting to get away from the classroom, from school, from the playground, to 'shut the door hard' on the brutality of the external world, to shut the self away in security. Such can be the power of a single word.

The above conversation was recorded ten years ago and these children are now young people of sixteen. The comprehensive school they go to is often in the local press. Mounted police officers sometimes stand guard at the school entrance to deter the gangs of white and Bangladeshi youths from taking baseball bats to one another. Could it be that Aysha has stopped shutting the door, that Farzana's little brother has decided the streets are as much his as anyone else's and that Iqbal no longer finds solace in silence? Ten years on, local schools and the community are living with the legacy of doing nothing about racism. Names can hurt every bit as much as sticks and stones, but in the end everyone involved becomes a victim of racism as Savitri Hensman (1994) eloquently illustrated in her poem, 'The Cage', in which the racist eagerly builds a cage in which to put 'the black' only to find, on completion, that he is inside too.

An inclusive multicultural curriculum would have created a positive linguistic environment for these British-Bangladeshi pupils and their white peers. Instead of confining them to narrow relationships bounded by a hostile language, school could have equipped all pupils with a language embedded in cooperative practice. The methodology of English as second language (EAL) specialists is particularly relevant here and can be applied in the teaching of all children (Richardson and Wood 1999).

Collaborative learning: cooperative power

Schools that fail to challenge racism and prejudice fail to equip pupils with the social, linguistic and intellectual skills to become fully educated citizens in a multi-ethnic society. Positive schools have an inclusive multicultural curriculum and an inclusive ethos. Many also have an inclusive pedagogy. By that I mean they apply theories of teaching and learning which recognise that education is fundamentally a social process. They view pupils as active agents in learning, not passive recipients of teaching, although the teacher is central to the process.

Our children in the above example knew only to well what it meant to have a teacher who lacked an authoritative presence in the classroom. An authoritative presence occurs when the teacher creates a purposeful environment for learning (DfEE 1998b: 13) in which there is mutual respect between pupils and teacher and between the pupils themselves. The teacher is in control of subject knowledge and uses her skill to structure the teaching of significant skills, concepts, facts and ideas in a logical sequence. Good classroom management, subject knowledge and planning are her generic attributes. An inclusive pedagogy is one in which the teacher's generic skills are used to engage pupils in collaborative talk and thought.

At the heart of collaboration between pupils is well-planned group work, which is designed to engage each member of the group in the collective pursuit of particular learning outcomes. Successful collaborative group work enables each pupil to simultaneously develop his or her language, thinking, self-concept and relationships. By means of heterogeneous grouping inclusive of gender, ability and ethnicity pupils begin to gain insights into one another that help to dispel stereotypes. Douglas Barnes (1976) was among the first educationalists to recognise that mixed ability grouping had positive linguistic and intellectual outcomes for all learners. I recall Year 4 pupils working as a group to evaluate each other's stories. They had been given a basic framework to guide their judgements. After each pupil had read their story, others in the group were invited to comment on aspects they liked and what advice they could give the writer. One girl with special needs gave her comments after a boy who was an EAL learner read his story. At the end she added, 'I think Rafiq's story is really good because it cannot be easy writing in English when it is not your first language'. Her insight, which was perhaps based on her own experiences with writing, demonstrated her ability to empathise with Rafiq. With insight came respect. Her comment served another purpose too. It enabled the teacher to perceive the girl differently, since empathy involves the psychological process of decentring.

Before they can take full advantage of the educational potential of collaborative learning, pupils need to acquire basic cooperative skills. These can be learned by means of time limited tasks in a variety of curriculum areas, starting with pair work and gradually progressing to larger groupings as pupils become more competent at managing group tasks. To ensure that group work integrates effective social interaction, purposeful talk and cognitive skills it requires careful planning, explicit explanation to pupils and well-structured activities. One example of a collaborative learning strategy I have extensively used is the jigsaw exercise. This strategy is particularly useful for introducing a topic or imparting a lot of information in a short space of time. I have used jigsaw exercises in two ways; with small groups and with whole classes.

In group activities each pupil has a fragment of information, which he or she contributes to the group. The task is complete when all pupils have pieced together all the fragments of information in order to solve a particular problem. Jigsaw exercises with the whole class begin in a similar way but each group has a fragment of information. When information is understood by each group member, pupils are re-grouped to include one pupil from each of the former groups. In the new group each pupil shares the fragment of information acquired in the previous group until a holistic 'picture' is produced. A variation of this is to allow pupils to move freely around the room to acquire fresh information from others after the initial group stage. Other examples of collaborative activities include brainstorming, barrier games, homing in, and collaborative drafting. A detailed explanation of these and other activities can be found in various sources (Brent Language Service 1999: 35–39; Ainscow 1999: 64–68; Coelho 1998: 134–146; Gardner in press). The Collaborative Learning Project (17 Barford Street, Islington, London N1 0QB, Director: Stuart Scott) has a wide range of teacher produced activities for different age groups and is an invaluable source of curriculum related materials.

Collaborative learning is both a useful pedagogic device and a powerful tool for empowering the learner. Drawing on evidence from elsewhere (Johnson and Johnson 1994; Slavin *et al.* 1984), Ainscow points out that collaborative practices can improve educational outcomes in terms of academic, social and psychological development. However, despite its value, collaborative learning it is not widely practised in schools (Ainscow 1999: 64). Given the prominence of group work in the National Literacy Strategy, collaborative practice needs to be an essential element in every teacher's repertoire of teaching methods.

Collaborative group work and the EAL learner

Collaborative practice has benefits for all learners but is especially useful to EAL pupils for a number of reasons. Firstly, it is a means of integrating EAL pupils, with varying degrees of English, into the mainstream classroom. Secondly, it puts curriculum related learning objectives at the centre of the process of language learning. The EAL pupil is simultaneously exposed to several language domains including: the language of social interaction and the language of the curriculum and curriculum related knowledge, concepts and skills (Brent Language Service 1999) Well organised collaborative group work creates a context in which pupils, including the EAL pupil, learn language because there is a real need to communicate. (Wiles 1981). Numerous studies have shown that talk-rich classrooms along the lines suggested above are the best environments for EAL acquisition (CRE 1986). Recent empirical study has demonstrated that achievement levels can be raised when talk becomes central to teaching and learning, especially when learning objectives take account of subject specific language, including technical vocabulary, language structure and linguistic functions and where these are modelled in teaching (Green 1999: 115–118).

Dulay *et al.* (1982) help to explain why this approach might be so successful. They have constructed a model of 'second' language acquisition in which conscious and subconscious processors of language operate. They identify three innate processors of language. Two of these, which they call the 'filter' and the 'organiser' operate subconsciously, leaving a third, the 'monitor', to process language at a conscious level. Readers will recognise the operation of the 'monitor' if they have ever had to use a foreign language of which they have only a partial grasp. The monitor is operating for the holidaymaker abroad when standing in a queue waiting to be served by a native speaker. As a speaker you are conscious of using language and are desperate not to make a mistake. The monitor rehearses the phrase you want to use, checking the vocabulary and syntax before you make an utterance.

For some individuals such self-consciousness is enough to inhibit their use of the second language. Dulay *et al.* refer to this as affective screening. High affective screening can slow down the rate of second language acquisition. In addition to personality traits, other factors such as age and environmental conditions can influence a learner's affective filter. Racial harassment, low teacher expectations and failure to value the speaker's first language can contribute to high affective screening. However, in classrooms where an inclusive pedagogy is evident and where there is a positive affective climate, leading to high levels of motivation, learning is most effective (Cooper and McIntyre 1996).

While Dulay *et al.* keep a place for the conscious learning of a second language, they suggest second language acquisition is more effective when the learner is relaxed and confident, causing the subconscious filters to operate. The brain's in-built structure subconsciously organises new language by identifying uniform patterns and by predicting correct forms of the language based on past exposure. Grammatical patterns are learned in a particular order which enables the learner to make closer and closer approximations to the correct use of the target language. Dulay *et al.* have referred to this process as the inter-language continuum. The initial stage of the inter-language continuum begins with a silent period, which can last from several weeks to several months. During this stage the learner begins 'tuning' in to the phonology of the language. When confronted with a new language little sense can be made of it until the learner can differentiate individual words and phrases. When the phonology of the target language is similar to the learner's first language this task is made easier, which may reduce the length of the silent period. Once the learner is able to recognise individual words an attempt is made to actively understand them. Nouns are usually learned early because they have a concrete referent. These are followed by verbs etc.

Dulay *et al.* add that second language acquisition is enhanced when learners work with their peers and people with whom they identify, particularly when language use is embedded in concrete activities. This is supported by research on mothers and their children, which found that when interactions were initiated by the child and were based on what was immediately apparent in the child's surroundings, the pace of the child's acquisition of language was better than when these conditions were absent (Wells 1987). Other research has shown how children and young peoples' language use can be inhibited when interacting with relatively unfamiliar adults in formal situations (Labov 1988). Initial speakers of an additional language can sometimes be seen conversing with their peers before they attempt utterances with adults.

Teachers can maximise the use of their EAL pupils' subconscious filters by creating learning conditions that generate natural communication and comprehensible contexts for language use. The less familiar the pupil is with the language to be learned the more context-embedded language use needs to be. Collaborative learning strategies, therefore, create the scaffolding necessary for language acquisition because talk takes place in relatively stress-free learning contexts. By listening to language use in such contexts teachers can often make better assessments of EAL pupils' knowledge of the target language than by other means.

From this discussion we can conclude that language acquisition and the order in which language is learned is due to innate mental processes, but that it is the learner who is actively engaged in making sense of new linguistic environments. However, the nature of the linguistic environment, in terms of how comprehensible new language is made for the learner, greatly influences the rate of the learner's additional language acquisition. This has important implications for both learners and teachers and impinges on the classroom climate in which they work.

The EAL learner and academic achievement

A distinction has been made between language used for everyday purposes and language used in the domain of the classroom. This distinction was initially conceptualised as the BICS/CALP dichotomy where BICS referred to basic inter-personal communication skills and CALP to cognitive and academic language (Cummins 1984). In addition to vocabulary, grammar and pronunciation, BICS includes the ability to use and comprehend the range of paralinguistic skills such as intonation, gesture, facial expression and body language, all of which are integral to a native speaker's communicative strategies. BICS was associated with skills in oracy.

According to Cummins's research a child might take up to two years to gain full native-like competence in the use of the second language for everyday purposes but up to a further five years to gain full communicative competence for academic purposes. An analysis of the syntactic differences between spoken and written English shows that some forms of curriculum related language are easier to acquire than others. Narrative shares some similarities with spoken English, which enables pupils as readers and writers to comprehend and to use its linguistic structures more easily than non-fiction writing, which tends to use such devices as the passive voice, complex sentences and subjunctive clauses (Perera 1984).

Initially, the processing of curriculum related language is more cognitively demanding for pupils, partly because of its more complex structure, but also because it is related to concepts and knowledge that are extensions or refinements of prior learning. In addition, a language develops in a social and cultural context. Learning a second language for academic purposes therefore involves being able to comprehend the socio-cultural semantic field which surrounds that language. Examples of socio-cultural semantic variables range from idioms through to religious and literary allusion. EAL learners who maintain their first language and develop higher order concepts in that language are better able to cope with CALP in languages added to their repertoire. The same point applies to EAL learners who are literate in their first language because they already possess a generic knowledge of literacy such as the principle of graphophonic representation.

Several implications arise from Cummins' BICS/CALP dichotomy. Firstly, it demonstrates that EAL learners are likely to have long-term needs. Linking EMTAG funding to National Curriculum results with a requirement to monitor achievement by ethnicity makes it possible to discern patterns in performance over the long term and to target resources accordingly. Support to fully access the curriculum will be a long-term need for a significant number of EAL pupils and resources should not be withdrawn once basic skills in English have been acquired.

Secondly, it raises the issue of assessment. There is a danger in assuming that fluency at the level of interpersonal communication for everyday purposes represents full fluency in the second language. Cummins shows this not to be the case by suggesting that fluency for academic purposes can take up to seven years. Teachers therefore need to guard against lowering their expectations of EAL pupils who do not attain on par with their monolingual peers. For this reason pupil records need to include information about the length of time the pupil has been learning English, as well as information about the pupil's knowledge of the first language, including levels of literacy. By means of detailed profiling of the learner's linguistic repertoire, together with assessment in the pupil's strongest language and consultation with parents about their perception of how the child is progressing, teachers are likely to gain a better insight into the pupil's potential to learn and achieve in English. Where a pupil's achievements do not match those of the peer group, profiling is likely to yield information that makes it possible to determine whether lack of progress is specifically due to some form of learning difficulty as opposed to EAL factors. We might expect that the proportion of EAL pupils with some form of Special Educational Need (SEN) will be similar to that for the population as a whole, which is estimated at 20 per cent (DES 1978).

Thirdly, Cummins' work forces us to consider the relationship of the demand of the curriculum on pupils, its associated language and the diverse needs of pupils in the class. While differentiation has become an accepted term in teachers' vocabulary, Cummins suggests learning activities must take account of cognitive load, types of language required and the EAL competence of the learner. Differentiated learning can be organised using a model of intersecting continua (see Figure 5.1).

Movement along the horizontal line determines the amount of language support given to the learner, ranging from completely context embedded support, which might include face-to-face interaction, visual clues and practical tasks, to no support at all, at the other end of the continuum. The vertical line denotes the cognitive load placed on the learner by the curriculum. The quadrants correlate levels of thought with differentiated support. Quadrant C is redundant because it offers no practical opportunities for learning and would include such things as rote learning and copying texts. Work for very able learners would be set in quadrant D (Hall 1995: 56). Pupils in the early stages of acquiring English require context embedded learning activities that do not require a high cognitive load. Learning should therefore be planned in quadrant A to ensure that language is both comprehensible and stress-free, thereby minimising risks of a high affective filter inhibiting language and cognitive development. As the pupil's competence in English increases learning moves along the vertical axis to quadrant B and ultimately to quadrant D. The model provides a strategic plan for curriculum delivery in multilingual classrooms.

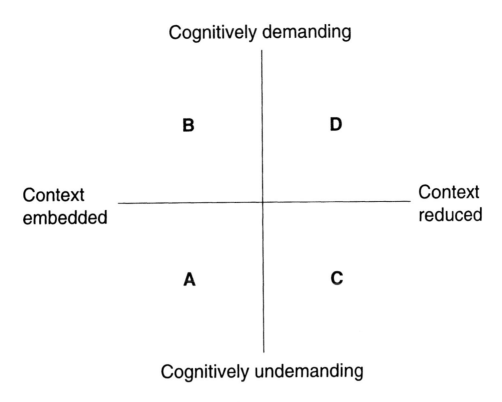

Figure 5.1 A model of intersecting continua

Hall (1995: 59–63) has given examples of the model's use to plan aspects of the National Curriculum in different Key Stages. Frederickson and Cline (1990) demonstrate the model's use for curriculum related assessment. Clearly, the model can be located within constructivist learning theory since its success depends upon identifying the pupil's potential to learn within a zone of proximal development (Vygotsky 1962). The zone of proximal development is the difference between a pupil's aided and unaided achievement. As the pupil moves through the quadrants, his or her zone of proximal development may alter. A pupil who made rapid progress in quadrant A and who received relatively little support may need to be reassessed for work in quadrants B and D where tasks and their related language become more demanding. Formative assessment related to work in these quadrants is likely to yield information that enables the teacher to properly scaffold learning for higher order cognitive and linguistic functions. Examples of the kind of cognitive and linguistic demands made of the pupil by the curriculum are given in Figure 5.2

A synthesis of Cummins' model with an aspect of Vygotskian theory, allied to the work of Dulay *et al.* and Wood *et al.*, provides the basis for a holistic

Cognitive demand	language	Cognitive demand	language
generalising	concrete nouns	predicting	terms and tenses expressing
	generic nouns		conditions
comparing and contrasting	adjectives	hypothesising	adjectives expressing
	adverbs of comparison		emotions
summarising	possessives	interpreting evidence	terms of cause and effect
	connectives		
planning	prepositions of time	evaluating	Examples:
			what would happen if . . .
classifying		analysing	what might be the cause of . . .
			as a result of . . .
recalling and reviewing		applying principles	it follows that
			therefore . . .
problem solving		justifying	
		developing argument	

Cognitive demand	language	
Locating information	concrete nouns	**Work in this quadrant would be**
	common adjectives	**context reduced and cognitively**
identifying	verbs – present	**undemanding. It would, therefore,**
naming	progressive	**have little or no relevance to learning.**
matching	adverbs	
retelling		
Transferring information		
Applying known procedures	Examples:	
describing observations	like, same as, different	
sequencing	similar, match, not alike . . .	

Figure 5.2 Cognitive and linguistic demands (A synthesis of Hall 1995: 57 and Brent Language Service, 1999: 41)

approach to teaching, learning and assessment in the multilingual classroom. Based on these theoretical constructs, teachers can plan for, and support, the cognitive and language development of their pupils, relating them to the progressive demands of National Curriculum programmes of study. Indeed, the use of language across the curriculum, which includes the specific functions of English relevant to particular subjects, is now a key element of the 'General teaching requirements' (DfEE/QCA 1999a: 38; DfEE/QCA 1999b: 40). Collaborative learning strategies provide a practical means of scaffolding pupils' cognitive and academic development while also enabling them to develop social skills. Good practice in the multilingual classroom must integrate these three elements (Brent Language Service 1999: 40). Where these elements are not integrated in teaching and learning there is a danger that not only might academic achievement be impaired but also inter-ethnic relationships could be grounded in hostile territory.

Language as social code

As previously stated, language is imbued with social significance. The way we pronounce words, the words we choose to use and the way we use them in everyday discourse convey social codes that signal social affiliation and social identity. Trudgill (1983) has documented the way in which language is a signifier of social class membership. Accent and dialect can situate us both socially and regionally. By referring to holidaymakers as 'emmets' (ants) the Cornish inhabitant instantly confirms his or her regional affiliation and psychologically excludes those outside the group.

As well as signifying regional affiliation and culture, language operates as an oral and aural marker of cultural identity for the speakers of Britain's 200 minority languages. The popularisation of regional accents through television soap operas and drama has contributed to our general awareness of language variation in Britain. The Liverpudlian habit of customising English, as in 'bezzie-mate' immediately locates the speaker for outsiders and conveys intimacy between Liverpudlians. Television has also introduced us to linguistic variation in youth culture, particularly the influence of 'Black-English.' The trend of semantic reversal is now well known. Current examples include; 'wicked', meaning fantastic and 'bad' meaning good. Asian languages too are beginning to make their mark through television. Those English speakers who have become cult followers of the comedy series 'Goodness Gracious Me' are fully conversant with what 'chudis' are, and what a dhunda is, by means of repetition of the phrases, 'kiss my chudis man' and 'so, how big is his dhunda?'

Language is part of the social fabric of our society. It is a binding thread between the individual and their community (Grugeon and Gardner 2000: 105). If we want education to reflect the kind of society we are, we also need to teach our pupils the social significance of the languages of our society. That means making them aware that language is situated in social interaction and is influenced by such things as the topic of conversation, the social relationship of the speakers and degrees of formality in social context (Halliday 1978). The basis for a coherent study of language is certainly signalled in the English programmes of study across all key stages (KS1 En1. 6a,b; KS2 En1 6a, b, c, DfEE/QCA 1999a; KS3 and 4 En1 6a-f DfEE/QCA 1999b). An understanding of the personal, social and cultural significance of language and varieties of English, including the dialect of Standard English, need to be part of every child's educational entitlement if young people are to be empowered as assertive and empathetic individuals who are able to establish and maintain positive relationships in a linguistically and culturally diverse society.

Summary

The current emphasis on the study of the constituent parts of English at the level of sounds, words, sentences and texts (DfEE1998c) is supplemented by a broader study of language in the National Curriculum. The inclusion of drama in the programmes of study for English provides teachers with a further arena in which language use and variation can be explored. In addition to differences between standard and other dialects of English, the study of language needs to be inclusive of linguistic diversity in the school, local community and society at large. The importance of language to individuals in terms of how it expresses their social and cultural identity needs to be taught alongside its importance as a highly symbolic means of communication.

There is also a place for the critical study of language. This would provide opportunities for pupils to explore the effect of particular words and phrases on people; to consider the power of language to affect emotional responses and people's lives. It needs to provide pupils with the insight to realise that a single word can have different meanings for different people. Ultimate empowerment occurs when pupils feel they have control of language rather than language being used as an instrument to control them. For some pupils who are the recipients of racist language, this means empowering them with the language to challenge oppressive uses of that language. Collaborative learning that engenders constructive talk around curriculum related and problem solving activities has been shown to improve language and academic development, and is one means by which pupils can develop their social skills and understanding of individual identities within and across gender, class and ethnicity.

Inclusive classrooms, founded on an inclusive curriculum, pedagogy and ethos could provide pupils with the multicultural understanding that is essential to the future well-being of our multi-ethnic society. The kind of society we want to be needs to be reflected in classroom practice and cannot be left to the rhetoric of policy. Classrooms are the theatres of educational policy where each and every player learns to take their place on the larger stage of adult life. Cooperative classrooms are likely to create cooperative citizens, but classrooms where children play out their prejudices are more than likely to produce angry, disenchanted and socially hostile individuals.

CHAPTER 6

Partnerships for learning

Learning may sometimes appear to be an individual act but, in essence, it is a social activity. Even the scholar working silently, surrounded by books, is engaged in a social act of learning. The books contain other people's ideas, propositions and arguments but by engaging with them the scholar is involved in silent dialogue with the minds of other scholars, which makes it, albeit indirectly, a social act. This depicts the fully independent learner, but classrooms contain more obvious examples of learning as a social act. One such example is collaborative learning, discussed in the previous chapter. Under the guidance of the teacher, positive partnerships between pupils can be developed to aid mutual learning. However, partnerships for learning can be extended beyond pupils to the adults who have a vested interest in learners.

This final chapter considers two further types of partnership that can be instrumental in making education a success. The active participation in education of parents and carers as the prime educators is recognised as a contributory factor to school effectiveness (Green 1999:150). However, multicultural schools often need to employ greater resourcefulness in order to initiate and maintain good lines of communication with parents (Blair *et al.* 1998: 143). For this reason, the job descriptions of many EMTAG staff include a home–school liaison brief, especially where bilingual skills are required. The chapter begins with an account of the school–parent liaison work conducted by Farida, an experienced bilingual classroom assistant. Farida's experience exemplifies the positive benefits of this aspect of her role but it also raises policy issues at school level. The second type of partnership dealt with is that between adults in the classroom. Teachers work with a variety of other adults, ranging from those temporarily involved in the learning of their pupils, such as guest speakers and theatre in education groups, to those adults with whom they have regular contact. Among this latter group are specialist teachers, classroom assistants and parent/carer helpers. Working in partnership with other adults in the classroom can have numerous benefits but only if both parties are clear about what needs to be done. The second part of the chapter considers some ground rules for effective working practices when two or more adults collaborate to make teaching and learning effective.

Partnerships between teachers and parents/carers

The link between academic achievement and parental interest in education has a long record in educational debate (Douglas 1964; Bastiani 1997). Real home–school partnerships help to create positive conditions for learning including; mutual support of children; improved self-esteem, confidence, motivation and independence. OFSTED (1993) noted the positive effect of home–school liaison in terms of pupils' improved confidence and progress, as well as greater involvement of parents in the work of the school.

Successive Education Acts have given parents a stronger role on school governing bodies and have enabled parents to have greater flexibility in their choice of school. In contrast to the past, when some schools actively discouraged parents beyond the school gates, parents are viewed as essential partners in the drive to raise standards. While parental involvement in education is keenly courted, it is not always easy to encourage at local level, nor is a simple causal relationship between increased parental involvement and academic achievement, universally accepted (Feuerstein 2000). A variety of factors can influence the extent to which parents become involved in their child's school and educational progress. Feuerstein draws on several studies to highlight the importance of such factors as social class, ethnic profile of the pupil population and staff, and the attitudes of teachers towards parents, in determining parental involvement. It has been suggested that as a function of cultural expectations some minority ethnic parents consider the teacher to be solely responsible for the education of their children (Siraj-Blatchford 1994, p.18). However, Kerbow and Bernhardt (1993 cited in Feuerstein 2000) found that schools with large minority populations were able to attract high levels of parental involvement. What is significant is the way in which schools approach parents to encourage their involvement. Farida demonstrates this point, but what is also evident from her comments is the need for a whole school approach to home–school liaison.

Farida's experience

The peripatetic nature of Farida's job afforded her little institutional status. Part of her job entailed liaison with parents at the beginning and end of the school day but not all the staff in the school was aware of the rationale for this aspect of her work. The following comments have been extracted from an interview with her based on her experience of working, over a three-year period, in a first school with an attached nursery.

> To begin with when parents came up to me staff thought I was just chatting, not doing my work.. They bring me things to give to the teacher, or ask me questions about the school. They do not ask the teacher. Mums want to ask questions about school . . . give me photo money, return things. They want to know how their child is getting on, so I tell them. It's taken me three years to get to this stage. I think when I am there parents feel more confident to approach school about things that concern them. It is better now but I still feel a little uncomfortable sometimes because they (the staff) look at me. I think, what are they thinking?

Many minority ethnic parents, for linguistic and cultural reasons, are more inhibited about talking to teachers than majority ethnic parents (Macbeth 1989 p. 166). Farida clearly performs an important function by providing a linguistic and cultural bridge between home and school. She understands the needs of parents and they respect her both as a member of their community and as a member of staff. Her very presence is the interface between what might otherwise be two disparate worlds, home and school. However, this is at some personal cost owing to the suspicions of colleagues who regard her as stepping over the boundary of her role. The aims and functions of home–school liaison staff need, therefore, to be transparent and part of a whole-school approach.

As well as encouraging parents to cross the threshold to school, Farida performs an important pastoral function through home visits and telephone contact.

> If a child has been away for three or four days, I do check to see if the child is O.K. . . . show we care. I make telephone calls too . . . if there is a meeting parents need to attend, I'll phone them . . . say, you should be there. Mrs. A has had four children at the school, the other day I phoned her about her fifth child entering Nursery . . . she turned up, she had never done that before.

With the support of the new teacher in-charge of the nursery, Farida felt more integral to the team but this was not replicated in main school.

> Mrs. H. and I plan our work together. It is less effective in main school than nursery . . . possibly because the children are older. There is less reason to contact parents, but still I do sometimes . . . mainly when children misbehave. I would say the majority of home visits and telephone calls home are related to misbehaviour. Teachers tend not to be aware of the role of the bilingual assistant. I think more communication is needed. Teachers need training, so they know

how to relate to minority ethnic children. If the teacher is cooperative, you can be effective, but some teachers are not cooperative.

Schools have their own cultures, created by the dynamic interplay of leadership style, collective values and institutional practices (Duignan 1989). Leadership style has an important impact on the ethos of home–school liaison (Macbeth 1989). The exercise of Farida's role was dependent upon positive practice being encouraged by leaders within the school. It was only with the active involvement of the new teacher in charge of nursery, that Farida was able to move the institution beyond its own boundary. Even so, it is evident that the institution was operating not on one boundary but two, with the nursery being far more flexible than main school. In highlighting the importance of *communication* and *training*, Farida pinpointed the crux of the problem. If home–school liaison is to be fully embedded in whole school practice the whole staff needs to understand its importance. This can only be achieved if time and resources are allocated to creating a corporate vision and common practices. While Farida was able to influence change with the support of the teacher in charge of nursery, permanent change will always be difficult without the support of senior managers. Likewise, good intentions will founder without teacher commitment and the right attitude. Farida observed double standards in the way teachers responded to parents.

> . . . some teachers are very nice.. they talk to parents, others are just unapproachable. Parents are scared of them. Some (teachers) seem very nice, but when parents have gone, they talk about them behind their backs, they are hypocritical. It all depends on their attitude.

Perhaps it is due to the attitudinal problems of some members of staff that Farida considers herself to be the 'gatekeeper' of the Muslim community's religious and cultural mores.

> Last week in nursery we made sandwiches with ham. The nursery staff know the Muslim children must not eat ham, but I was there, so parents know I wouldn't let the children eat the sandwiches. So they didn't mind them making them. Parents know children can always use their first language when they need to . . . or talk about their culture. More children speak in Panjabi at school now than before.

As this example demonstrates, Farida is a symbol of psychological and cultural security in an environment where religious taboos are blatantly disregarded. Effective though her work is, Farida does not have the full support of colleagues. In contrast, the two case study schools in Chapter Four took a proactive whole-school approach towards home–school liaison and were able to develop strong links with parents. There is a correlation between contact with parents and parental interest in school; the more parents are contacted, the more they tend to participate in the life of the school (Feuerstein 2000). For schools generally, but particularly the multi-cultural school, home–school liaison has to be grounded in effective two-way communication. Across what is often a cultural-linguistic divide common ground needs to be established between schools and parents in order to achieve two objectives. Firstly, the dissemination to parents of educational aims, objectives and pedagogy, and, secondly to inform teachers of parental expectations, cultural and religious mores, linguistic diversity and the breadth of pupils' experiences. The divide between teachers and parents is often bridged by the bilingual assistant, who resides in a bi-cultural 'field' and who possesses the requisite knowledge to span the gap between the respective cultures and languages of home and school.

Partnerships in the classroom

The image of the teacher working in solitary isolation with a class of pupils is more appropriate in the archives than in the modern school. Continual change in educa-tion since the Education Reform act of 1988 has forced teachers everywhere to work more collegially in order to share ideas and solve problems. There has also been a dramatic increase in the number of associate staff in schools. On average a primary school has 5 non-teaching staff, while the number in secondary schools is 14 (Howson 2000). Schools with EMTAG funding will have additional staff, both teachers and non-teachers. The increased likelihood that class teachers will work with other adults in the classroom has had an impact on generic teaching skills, which now includes the ability to take account of others when planning and managing teaching and learning. Indeed, the requirement to establish effective working relationships with professional colleagues and associate staff is now a prerequisite for Qualified Teacher Status (DfEE 1998b: Annex A: Db).

Farida talked briefly about her work with colleagues in the classroom, which varied according to the attitude of the teacher. I asked her if she was included in planning meetings. She said: 'In Nursery, every Wednesday. I'm only there on a Wednesday, so they have the meeting when I'm there. It has only happened recently, since Mrs. H. took over.' However, the inclusion of Farida as an integral member of the teaching and support team was not replicated in the main school: 'There (main school) the teachers direct what I do . . . some are cooperative . . . if I think something isn't working and suggest something different, they'll listen . . . but one teacher in particular says, I am the teacher . . . you do what I say.'

Bilingual colleagues can make significant contributions to learning. They have linguistic skills and bi-cultural understanding that can unlock the potential of bilingual pupils, as well as enhance the social and cultural development of the whole class, including the teacher, in some instances. The use of such expertise should not be left to chance, or discouraged by a disparaging comment.

Planning for partnership

Like home–school liaison, partnerships in the classroom need to be part of a systematic whole-school approach underpinned by careful management. We might view such management as operating at two levels; the level of the school and the level of the classroom. In both cases an essential aspect of management is communication. At school level, aims and purposes of adults working together in the classroom need to be transparent so that there is no ambiguity among staff. Such purposes might include staff and curriculum development or additional support for pupils in order to achieve particular learning goals. The importance of monitoring pupil achievement and targeting human resources in order to raise attainment levels of under-achieving groups has been discussed in previous chapters but colleagues need to be clear about the reasons why some classes are receiving support while others are not. A failure to inform, supported by verifiable data compiled from assessment records, may lead to resentment among colleagues who do not receive additional help in the first instance. Staff are more likely to accept a strategic plan, even though they might not be directly involved, if they have had an opportunity to contribute to the thinking behind the process. Agreement about goals and discussion about strategies to achieve those goals can involve all staff in designated staff meetings and help to give colleagues a sense of being part of a shared project. The Partnership Teaching pack (Bourne and McPake 1991) is a useful resource for whole-school in-service training and is especially designed for multicultural schools with EMTAG staff.

A framework for partnership

Once it is clear where additional adult help is to be targeted, the process of defining roles and responsibilities in the classroom can begin. This is probably best achieved by the class teacher, who has direct experience of the class, and the additional adult, planning together. In the early stages, sufficient time will be required for the two colleagues to develop a good working relationship. Invariably, this will involve colleagues sharing their knowledge, experience and educational philosophy. Even when colleagues have similar professional outlooks, it is likely that they will learn a great deal from one another during the course of the partnership. For this reason partnership teaching is an invaluable means of professional development. The use of a framework around which to build an effective partnership is likely to guide colleagues through the early stages and speed up the process of defining the *modus operandi*. If clear goals are established from the outset minds can be concentrated on viable means to achieve desired outcomes. At the heart of any partnership in the classroom is the aim to improve the quality and effect of teaching and learning.

The framework for developing effective partnerships outlined below is based on Bourne and McPake's (1991) Partnership Cycle and includes six phases:

- identification of pupils and their needs;
- target setting;
- planning;
- teaching;
- evaluation;
- reporting and dissemination.

Identification of pupils and their needs
Schools with effective systems of assessment, recording and monitoring are readily able to identify groups of pupils requiring additional support. Annual records of QCA test results, SATs and teacher assessments provide a broad picture of attainment. They make it easier to identify pupils who are under-achieving relative to their peer group and the expected level of attainment for their Key Stage. However, this information only gives a broad-brush stroke and finer detail is required in order to target resources purposefully at classroom level. The class teacher's own records and informal assessments of pupils will complete the picture. They will help to identify the aspects of particular attainment targets and which pupils require additional support. In addition to records of attainment, the class teacher's knowledge of each pupil's affective response to learning will help to identify need.

Target setting
Targets for individual pupils and groups of pupils are likely to be dependent upon three factors: the identified needs of pupils; the medium term curriculum plan and the agreed time period for the partnership. Clearly a coincidence of pupil need and the content and learning objectives in the medium term plan will frame the range of possible targets, but the simple question of what is achievable within the time available is likely to pinpoint realistic teaching and learning targets for the partnership.

Planning
At the heart of the planning process will be the learning needs of pupils in relation to the linguistic and cognitive demand of the curriculum. In conjunction with the specific learning objectives for the lesson and the longer-term targets for pupils, these factors will concentrate minds on relevant materials and resources and

particular teaching methods and strategies to employ in the classroom. The two colleagues in the partnership need to agree on specific roles and responsibilities so there is no confusion over who is doing what. Responsibilities might cover preparation for the lesson or parts of it, including the collection or making of resources. Decisions need to be made about which colleague will be responsible for teaching and assessing particular pupils or whether both will take dual responsibility for the whole class. The planning stage also provides colleagues with the opportunity to share expertise in order to agree on particular teaching and learning strategies they think will prove effective. In multilingual classrooms, languages other than English can be an asset to learning. The linguistic expertise of bilingual adults therefore is a valuable resource and should be used to help pupils acquire and consolidate concepts.

Teaching

During the lesson, teacher colleagues might switch between taking the lead and assisting the other in lesson delivery. Whatever agreement has been reached at the planning stage needs to be communicated to pupils along with learning objectives so that learners themselves are clear about teachers' roles and responsibilities. Working in partnership obviously gives pupils more adult contact but it also enables both adults more time to monitor learning and to liaise during the lesson. One colleague may miss what the other sees but by talking to one another during the lesson a more comprehensive view of what is being learnt can be achieved, which could have an effect on the direction of the lesson. This should enable the two colleagues to modify their plans and fine tune their teaching to meet freshly observed pupil needs. By sharing information about pupils' progress colleagues are able to gain insights into pupils' levels of understanding and thereby improve assessment data.

Evaluation

In addition to liaison within the lesson, time is required to fully evaluate the effectiveness of teaching on learning. In giving feedback to one another colleagues will want to make judgements about teaching methods and strategies. This could prove sensitive, particularly if scrutiny falls on part of the lesson for which one colleague took sole responsibility. However, from the outset, it should be clear to everyone involved that partnerships in the classroom are professional relationships, and that colleagues are acting as critical friends for one another. In the end it is not egos that are at stake but the learning of pupils. The outcome of the evaluation should therefore inform future lesson planning in order to take pupils' learning further.

Reporting and dissemination

In order to maintain a whole-school perspective on classroom partnerships, opportunities to report back to staff on the progress of teaching and learning need to be arranged. Records of joint lesson evaluations will enable the two colleagues in the partnership to report accurately on what proved effective and what did not. Other colleagues can be informed of particular resources, methods and strategies that helped pupils' learning. In this way, the specific classroom partnership can be used to spread knowledge and expertise across the school, which should enable other colleagues to draw from a wider repertoire of teaching strategies when planning their own lessons.

End note

While the outline above is intended for partnerships between class teachers and other professional or associate staff, it can be modified to include parents or other helpers. Parents, carers and other family members possess numerous skills and talents that can be utilised in the classroom. However, what may make them different from professional and associate colleagues is their lack of detailed knowledge of the curriculum and teaching methods. Some schools have sought to overcome this drawback by providing training sessions for adult helpers before they begin supporting in the classroom. As with all working relationships two-way communication is essential to developing a rapport. Armed with a knowledge of the adult's particular strengths and expertise, the class teacher can negotiate a role that will give the partner a sense of purpose. The work of classroom assistants and parent helpers is most likely to be targeted at particular groups of pupils following an input by the teacher. Working with the group the adult helper can advance understanding by stimulating thinking and discussion of the key points of the lesson. In order to do so the adult helper will need to be clear about the learning objectives, concepts and subject specific vocabulary that are central to the lesson. As with other partnerships, teacher–parent partnerships must serve the primary objective of enhancing pupils' learning.

Glossary

BICS/CALP
The acronym BICS/CALP first appeared in the early work of the Canadian linguist Jim Cummins. BICS stands for Basic Interpersonal Communication Skills and refers to the type of language used for normal spoken everyday social interaction. Cummins makes the distinction between this type of language and the ability to use language to achieve academic success, which he called Cognitive and Academic Language Proficiency. Cummins later modified what came to be known as the BICS/CALP dichotomy because it implied that all spoken language was invariably less cognitively demanding than CALP, which had been associated with written language.

EAL
English as an Additional Language. The term is applied to speakers of other languages who are learning, or have learnt, English. In the 1990s it replaced an earlier term English as a Second Language (ESL) to signify the fact that a significant number of people are multilingual and that English may be their third, fourth or fifth language.

EMTAG
Ethnic Minority and Traveller Achievement Grant. This was formerly known as Section 11 Grant, but when its administration was transferred to the DfEE from the Home Office, the grant became a sub-fund of the Standards Fund.

Fte   Full-time equivalent.

LMS

The Local Management of Schools is a generic term that refers to the devolution of budgets and decision-making to individual schools. Before LMS, educational policy and budgets were administered by Local Education Authorities.

MFL   Modern Foreign Language.

NLS   National Literacy Strategy.

MASS   Minority Achievement Support Service.

PANDA

The term stands for performance and assessment. Ofsted produces an annual document in which each school's characteristic and SATs result is contextualised against national data and the performance of similar schools. Individual schools use this contextualised data in order to measure their relative success and to set future targets for improvement.

SMSC

The acronym stands for Spiritual, Moral, Social and Cultural development of pupils, a cross-curricular theme.

SHAP

SHAP is not an acronym but a signifier for the Working Party on World Religions in Education. The working party was established in 1969 at a conference held at the Shap Wells Hotel in Cumbria.

References

Ainscow, M. (1999) *Understanding the Development of Inclusive Schools.* London: Falmer Press.

Anderson, G. and Arsenault, N. (1998) *Fundamentals of Educational Research.* London: Falmer Press.

Angelou, M. (1984) *I Know Why the Caged Bird Sings.* London: Virago.

Barnes, D. (1976) *From Communication to Curriculum.* Harmondsworth: Penguin Books.

Bassey, M. (1995) *Creating Education Through Research.* Newark: Kirklington Moor Press in association with the British Educational Research Association.

Bastiani, J. ed. (1997) *Home–School Work in Multi-cultural Settings.* London: David Fulton Publishers.

Bhatti, G. (1999) *Asian Children at Home and at School: An Ethnographic Study.* London: Routledge.

Blair, M. *et al.*(1998) *Making the Difference: Teaching and Learning Strategies in Successful Multi-ethnic Schools.* Norwich: HMSO.

Bolton, E.J. (1979) Education in a Multiracial Society, *Trends in Education*, 4, 3–7.

Bourdieu, P. and Passerton, J.C. (1977) *Reproduction in Education, Society and Culture.* London: Sage.

Bourne, J. and McPake, J. (1991) *Partnership Teaching: Cooperative teaching strategies for English language support in multilingual classrooms.* London: HMSO.

Braithwaite, E. (1978) *Reluctant Neighbours.* London: New English Library.

Brent Language Service (1999) *Enriching Literacy – Text, Talk and Tales in Today's Classroom: A Practical Handbook for Multilingual Schools.* Stoke-on-Trent: Trentham Books.

Brown, B. (1998) *Unlearning Discrimination in the Early Years.* Stoke-on-Trent: Trentham Books.

Chadwick, N. (1970) *The Celts*. Harmondsworth: Penguin Books.

Coard, B. (1971) *How the West Indian Child is made Educationally Subnormal in the British School: The Scandal of the Black Child in Schools in Britain*. London: Beacon Books.

Coelho, E. (1998) *Teaching and Learning in Multicultural Schools*. Clevedon: Multilingual Matters.

Cohen, L. and Cohen, A. (eds) (1986) *Multicultural Education: A Sourcebook for Teachers*. London: Harper and Row.

Cohen, L. *et al.* (2000) *Research Methods in Education*, 5th edn. London: Routledge Falmer.

Collings, P. (1999) 'Schools in deprived areas,' in Chitty, C. and Dunfold, J. (eds) *State Schools: New Labour and the Conservative Legacy*. London: Woburn Press.

Cooper, P. and McIntyre, D. (1996) *Effective Teaching and Learning*. Buckingham: Open University Press.

CRE (1986) *Teaching English as a Second Language: Report of a Formal Investigation in Calderdale Local Education Authority*. London: Commission for Racial Equality.

CRE (1989) *Code of Practice for the Elimination of Racial Discrimination in Education*. London: Commission for Racial Equality.

CRE (1996) *Roots of The Future: Ethnic Diversity in the Making of Britain*. London: Commission for Racial Equality.

Cummins, J. (1984) *Bilingualism and Special Education: Issues in Assessment and Pedagogy*. Clevedon: Multilingual Matters.

Darke, M. (1978) *A Long Way To Go*. Harmondsworth: Kestrel Books.

Delamont, S. (1992) *Fieldwork in Educational Settings: Methods, Pitfalls and Perspectives*. London: Falmer Press.

DES (1965) Circular 7/65 *The Education of Immigrants*. London: HMSO.

DES (1974) *Educational Disadvantage and the Educational Needs of Immigrants: Observations on the Report on Education of the Select Committee on Race Relations and Immigration*. London: HMSO.

DES (1978) *Report of the Committee of Enquiry into Special Educational Needs (The Warnock Report)*. London: HMSO.

DES (1989) *National Curriculum: From Policy To Practice*. Stanmore: Department of Education and Science.

DFE (1995) *Key Stages 1 and 2 of the National Curriculum*. London: HMSO.

DfEE (1998a) *Letter to CEOs*, 27th October 1998.

DfEE (1998b) *Teaching: High Status, High Standards*. London: Department of Education and Employment.

DfEE (1998c) *The National Literacy Strategy*. London: DfEE.

DfEE (1999a) *Supplement to Circular 13/98 The Standards Fund 1999–2000*. London: DfEE.

DfEE (1999b) *Circular 16/99 The Standards Fund 2000–2001*. London: DfEE.

DfEE/QCA (1999a) *The National Curriculum: Handbook for primary teachers in England www.nc.uk.net – Key Stages 1 and 2*. London: DfEE/QCA.

DfEE/QCA (1999b) *The National Curriculum: Handbook for secondary teachers in England www.nc.uk.net – Key Stages 3 and 4*. London: DfEE/QCA.

DfEE (2000a) *Grammar for Writing*. London: DfEE.

DfEE (2000b) *Removing the Barriers: Raising Achievement Level for Minority Ethnic Pupils – Key Points for Schools*. London: DfEE.

Dhondy, F. (1976) *East End at Your Feet*. Basingstoke: Macmillan Education.

Douglas, J.W.B. (1964) *The Home and the School*. London: MacGibbon and Kee.

Duignan, P.A.. (1989) Reflective Management: the key to quality leadership, in Riches, C. and Morgan, C. eds. *Human Resource Management in Education*. Milton Keynes: Open University Press.

Dulay, H. *et al.* (1982) *Lanuage Two*. Oxford: Oxford University Press.

Dummett, A. (1985) 'From immigrants to ethnic minorities', *Multicultural Teaching, to Combat Racism in School and Community*, 3(2) Spring 1985.

Feuerstein, A. (2000) 'School characteristics and parent involvement: influences on participation in children's schools'. *The Journal of Educational Research*, **94**(1).

Focus in Education Productions and Elmhurst County First School (1994) *Home – The Starting Point: Under 5's and their Preparation for School*. Thames Ditton: Focus in Education Productions.

Foucault, M. (1980) Two Lectures, in *Power/Knowledge: Selected Interviews and Other Writings*. New York: Pantheon.

Frederickson, N. and Cline, T. (1990) *Curriculum Related Assessment with Bilingual Children: a set of working papers*. London: UCL.

Fryer, P. (1984) *Staying Power: The History of Black People in Britain*. London: Pluto Press.

Gaine, C. (1988) *No Problem Here: A Practical Approach to Education and 'Race' in White schools*. London: Hutchinson.

Gaine, C. and George, R. (1999) *Gender, 'Race' and Class in Schooling*. London: Falmer Press.

Gardner, P. (1987) *A Short Ethno-linguistic Study of Bilingualism* (unpublished).

Gardner, P. (in press) *Strategies and Resources for Teaching and Learning in Multicultural Classrooms*. London: David Fulton Publishers.

Gibson, M. (1988) *Accommodation without Assimilation*. Ithaca and London: Cornell University Press.

Gill, D. and Levidow, L. (1987) *Anti-racist Science Teaching*. London: Free Association Books.

Gillborn, D. and Gipps, C. (1996) *Recent Research on the Achievements of Ethnic Minority Pupils, OFSTED Reviews of Research*. London: HMSO.

Gillborn, D. and Mirza, H. (2000) *Educational Inequality: Mapping Race, Class and Gender – A Synthesis of Research Evidence.* London: OFSTED.

Green, P. (1999) *Raise the Standard: A practical guide to raising ethnic minority and bilingual pupils' achievement.* Stoke-on-Trent: Trentham Books.

Grinter, R. (1985) 'Bridging the Gulf: the need for Anti-Racist Multicultural Education', *Multicultural Teaching,* 3(2) Spring 1985, 7–10.

Grugeon, E. and Gardner, P. (2000) *The Art of Storytelling for Teachers and Pupils: Using Stories to Develop Literacy in Primary Classrooms.* London: David Fulton Publishers.

Gundara, J. (2000) 'Expect good – not good enough', *The Teacher,* July/August 2000: 13.

Guy, Rosa (1982) *The Friends.* London: Macmillan.

Hall, D. (1995) *Assessing the Needs of Bilingual Pupils: Living in Two Languages.* London: David Fulton Publishers.

Halliday, M.A.K. (1978) *Language as Social Semiotic: The Social Interpretation of Language and Meaning.* London: Edward Arnold.

Hammersley, M. (1989) *The Dilemma of Qualitative Method: Herbert Blumer and the Chicago Tradition.* London: Routledge.

Hammersley, M. and Atkinson, P. (1983) *Ethnography: Principles in Practice.* London: Tavistock.

Hensman, S. (1994) 'The Cage', in Bhindu, M. *Jumping Across Worlds: An Anthology of International Poetry.* NATE.

Hill, C. (1991) *The World Turned Upside Down: Radical Ideas during the English Revolution.* London: Penguin.

Hill, R. and Bell, A. (1988) *The Other Face of Terror: Inside Europe's Neo-Nazi Network.* London: Grafton Books.

Hitchcock, G. and Hughes, D. (1995) *Research and the Teacher: A Qualitative Introduction to School-based Research,* 2nd edn. London: Routledge.

Howson, J. (2000) 'Rise and rise of support army', *TES,* 8th December.

ILEA (1981) *Education in a Multiethnic Society: An Aide-memoire for the Inspectorate.* London: ILEA.

ILEA (1983a) *Race, Sex and Class 2. Multi-Ethnic Education in Schools.* London: ILEA.

ILEA (1983b) *Race, Sex and Class 3. A Policy for Equality: Race.* London: Inner London Education Authority.

ILEA (1983c) *Race, Sex and Class 4. Anti-Racist Statements and Guidelines.* London: ILEA.

ILEA (1985) *Everyone Counts: looking for bias and insensitivity in primary mathematics materials.* London: ILEA Centre for Learning Resources.

Jeffcoate, R. (1979) *Positive Image: Towards a Multiracial Curriculum.* London: Writers and Readers Publishing Cooperative.

Johnson, D.W. and Johnson, R.T. (1994) *Learning Together and Alone.* Boston: Allyn and Bacon.

Jones, R. (2000) 'Out of the Abyss: The current state of multicultural education in primary education', *Education 3–13,* March 2000.

Kerbow, D. and Bernhardt, A. (1993) Parent intervention in the school: The context of minority involvement. In Cioleman, J. and Schneider, B. (eds) *Parents, their Children and Schools.* Boulder: Westview.

Kincheloe, J.L. and Steinberg, S.R. (1997) *Changing Multiculturalism.* Buckingham: Open University Press.

Labov, W. (1988) 'The logic of non-standard English', in Mercer, N. (ed.) *Language and Literacy From an Educational Perspective – Volume 1 Language Studies.* Milton Keynes: Open University Press.

Macbeth, A. (1989) *Involving Parents: Effective Parent-Teacher Relations.* London: Heinemann.

Macdonald, I. (1989) *Murder in the Playground: The Report of the Macdonald Inquiry into Racism and Racial Violence in Manchester Schools.* London: Lonsight Press.

Macpherson, W. (1999) *The Stephen Lawrence Inquiry.* London: The Stationery Office.

Mandela, N. (1994) *Long Walk to Freedom: The Autobiography of Nelson Mandela,* London: Little, Brown and Company.

Maslow, A.H. (1976) *The Farther Reaches of Human Nature.* Harmondsworth: Penguin.

Mirza, H. (1995) 'The Myth of Underachievement', in Dawtrey, L. *et al.* (eds.), *Equality and Inequality in Education Policy.* Clevedon: Multilingual Matters in association with The Open University.

Mullard, C. (1984) *Anti-racist Education: A Theoretical Basis,* NAME Conference 1984.

Needle, J. (1979) *My Mate Shofiq.* London: William Collins.

Nehaul, K. (1996) *The Schooling of Children of Caribbean Heritage.* Stoke-on-Trent: Trentham Books.

OFSTED (1993) *Education Support for Minority Ethnic Communities: a review of schools April 1922–November 1993.*

OFSTED (1997) *The Assessment of the Language Development of Bilingual Pupils.* London: OFSTED Publications.

OFSTED (1999) *Raising the Attainment of Minority Ethnic Pupils – School and LEA Responses.* London: OFSTED.

Panayi, P. (1999) *The Impact of Immigration: A documentary history of the effects and experiences of immigrants in Britain since 1945.* Manchester: Manchester University Press.

Perera, K. (1984) *Children's Writing and Reading: Analysing Classroom Language.* Oxford: Blackwell in association with Deutsch.

Rampton, A. (1981) *West Indian Children in our Schools: Interim Report of the Committee of Inquiry into the Education of Children from Ethnic Minority Groups.* London: HMSO.

Richardson, R. and Wood, A. (1999) *Inclusive Schools, Inclusive Society: Race and Identity on the Agenda.* Stoke-on-Trent: Trentham Books.

Rosen, H. (1988) The Voices of Communities and Language in Classrooms: A review of *Ways with Words,* in Mercer, N. (ed.) *Language and Literacy from an Educational Perspective* 2 Milton Keynes: Open University Press.

Runnymede Tust (1993) *Equality Assurance In Schools.* Stoke-on-Trent: Trentham Books.

SCAA (1996) *Teaching English as an Additional Language: A Framework for Policy.* Hayes: School Curriculum and Assessment Authority.

SHAP Working Party (1999) *SHAP Calendar of Religious Festivals,* London: SHAP Working Party C/O National Society's RE Centre, 36 Causton St. London SW1P 4AU.

Siraj-Blatchford, I. (1994) *The Early Years: Laying the Foundations for Racial Equality.* Stoke-on-Trent: Trentham Books.

Sivanadan, A. (2000) 'Reclaiming the struggle – one year on', *Multicultural Teaching* 18(2) Spring 2000.

Slavin, R.E. (1984) 'Effects of cooperative learning and individualized instruction in mainstreamed students', *Exceptional Children,* 50(5), 434–443.

Soyinka, W. (1970) in Lomax, A. and Abdul, R. (eds) *3000 Years of Black Poetry: an Anthology.* New York: Dodd, Mead and Co.

Smith, R. (1982) *Sumitra's Story.* London: Bodley Head.

Spender, D. (1982) *Invisible Women: The Schooling Scandal.* London: Writers and Readers Cooperative.

Swann, M. (1985) *Education For All: The Report of the Committee of Inquiry into the Education of Children from Ethnic Minority Groups.* London: HMSO.

Taylor, M.D. (1977) *Roll of Thunder Hear My Cry.* Harmondsworth: Puffin.

Thompson, E.P. (1991) *The Making of the English Working Class.* London: Penguin.

Tomlinson, S. (1983) *Ethnic Minorities in British Schools.* London: Heinemann.

TTA/CRE (1998) *Teaching in Multi-Ethnic Britain: A Joint Report by the Teacher Training Agency and the Commission for Racial Equality.* London: TTA/CRE.

TTA (2000) *Raising the Attainment of Minority Ethnic Pupils.* London: Teacher Training Agency.

Trudgill, P. (1983) *Sociolinguistics: an Introduction to Language and Society.* London: Penguin.

Visram, R. (1995) *The History of the Asian Community in Britain.* Hove: Wayland Publishers.

Vygotsky, L. (1962) *Thought and Language.* Cambridge, Mass: MIT Press.

Weiner, G. (1994) *Feminisms in Education.* Buckingham: Open University Press.
Wells, G. (1987) *The Meaning Makers.* London: Hodder and Stoughton.
Wiles, S. (1981) Language Issues in the Multicultural Classroom, in Mercer, N. (ed.) *Language in School and Community.* London: Edward Arnold.
Wood, D. (1998) *How Children Think and Learn* 2nd edn. Oxford: Blackwell.

Web sites:

Home Office Section II grant – http://www.homeoffice.gov.uk/reu/grant.htm
Qualifications and Curriculum Authority – www.qca.org.uk

Addresses:

Collaborative Learning Project: Director, Stuart Scott, 17 Barford Street, Islington, London N1 0QB. Tel/Fax: 020 7226 8885.

Author index

Subject index